Securing SCADA Systems

Securing SCADA Systems

Ronald L. Krutz

Wiley Publishing, Inc.

Securing SCADA Systems

Published by
Wiley Publishing, Inc.
10475 Crosspoint Boulevard
Indianapolis, IN 46256
www.wiley.com

Copyright © 2006 by Wiley Publishing, Inc., Indianapolis, Indiana

Published simultaneously in Canada

ISBN-13: 978-0-7645-9787-9
ISBN-10: 0-7645-9787-6

For general information on our other products and services or to obtain technical support, please contact our Customer Care Department within the U.S. at (800) 762-2974, outside the U.S. at (317) 572-3993 or fax (317) 572-4002.

Library of Congress Cataloging-in-Publication Data

Krutz, Ronald L., 1938–
  Securing SCADA systems / Ronald L. Krutz.
       p. cm.
  Includes bibliographical references and index.
  ISBN-13: 978-0-7645-9787-9 (cloth : alk. paper)
  ISBN-10: 0-7645-9787-6 (cloth : alk. paper)
  1. Process control. 2. Data protection. 3. Computer security. I. Title.
  TS156.8.K78 2005
  670.42'7558—dc22
                          2005026371

To Emma Antoinette:

*The latest Lady Love in my life—a precious beauty—
and only 18 months old.*

*Love
Grandpapa*

About the Author

Ronald L. Krutz, Ph.D., P.E., CISSP, ISSEP, is a senior information security researcher for Lockheed Martin Information Technology. In this capacity, he works with a team responsible for advancing the state of the art in information systems security. He has more than 40 years of experience in distributed computing systems, computer architectures, real-time systems, information assurance methodologies, and information security training.

He has been an information security consultant at REALTECH Systems Corporation and BAE Systems, an associate director of the Carnegie Mellon Research Institute (CMRI), and a professor in the Carnegie Mellon University Department of Electrical and Computer Engineering. Dr. Krutz founded the CMRI Cybersecurity Center and was founder and director of the CMRI Computer, Automation, and Robotics Group. He is also a distinguished special lecturer in the Center for Forensic Computer Investigation at the University of New Haven, a part-time instructor in the University of Pittsburgh Department of Electrical and Computer Engineering, and a registered professional engineer.

Dr. Krutz is the author of seven best-selling publications in the area of information systems security, and is a consulting editor for John Wiley & Sons for its information security book series. He holds B.S., M.S., and Ph.D. degrees in electrical and computer engineering.

Credits

Executive Editor
Carol Long

Development Editor
Tom Dinse

Production Editor
Kathryn Duggan

Copy Editor
Maarten Reilingh

Editorial Manager
Mary Beth Wakefield

Production Manager
Tim Tate

Vice President and Executive Group Publisher
Richard Swadley

Vice President and Executive Publisher
Joseph B. Wikert

Project Coordinator
Ryan Steffen

Graphics and Production Specialists
Karl Brandt
Carrie A. Foster
Stephanie D. Jumper
Barbara Moore

Quality Control Technicians
Jessica Kramer
Robert Springer

Proofreading and Indexing
TECHBOOKS Production Services

Contents

Acknowledgments

Special thanks to my wife, Hilda, for her encouragement and support during yet another book project.

I also want to thank Carol A. Long, executive acquisitions editor, Networking and Security, Wiley Technology Publishing, for her support and advice on this text and Tom Dinse, development editor, Wiley Publishing, for his excellent editing efforts.

Special Acknowledgment

I want to express my appreciation to Dr. Eric Cole, chief scientist at Lockheed Martin Information Technologies, for his input to this text as a subject matter expert.

Dr. Cole is a renowned thought leader with over 15 years of experience in the network-security consulting market space, with clients including leading international banks, Fortune 500 companies, and the CIA. Eric is a member of the HoneyNet project and the CVE editorial board, and is a recognized author of several books, including *Hackers Beware* and *Hiding in Plain Sight*.

Introduction

Computer-based supervisory control and data acquisition (SCADA) systems have evolved over the past 40 years, from standalone, compartmentalized operations into networked architectures that communicate across large distances. In addition, their implementations have migrated from custom hardware and software to standard hardware and software platforms. These changes have led to reduced development, operational, and maintenance costs as well as providing executive management with real-time information that can be used to support planning, supervision, and decision making. These benefits, however, come with a cost. The once semi-isolated industrial control systems using proprietary hardware and software are now vulnerable to intrusions through external networks, including the Internet, as well as from internal personnel. These attacks take advantage of vulnerabilities in standard platforms, such as Windows, and PCs that have been adopted for use in SCADA systems.

This situation might be considered a natural progression of moderate concern—as in many other areas using digital systems—if it were not for the fact that these SCADA systems are controlling a large percentage of the United States' and the world's critical infrastructures, such as nuclear power plants, electricity generating plants, pipelines, refineries, and chemical plants. In addition, they are directly and indirectly involved in providing services to seaports, transportation systems, pipelines, manufacturing plants, and many other critical enterprises.

A large body of information-system security knowledge has accumulated concerning the protection of various types of computer systems and networks. The fundamental principles inherent in this knowledge provide a solid foundation for application to SCADA systems. However, some of the characteristics, performance requirements, and protocols of SCADA system components require adapting information-system security methods in industrial settings.

In order to present a complete view of SCADA system security concepts and their important role in the nation's critical infrastructure, this text begins by defining SCADA system components and functions, and providing illustrations of general SCADA systems architectures. With this background, specific SCADA implementations in a variety of critical applications are presented along with a determination of security concerns and potential harmful outcomes of attacks on these operations.

The text follows these illustrations with a detailed look at the evolution of SCADA protocols and an overview of the popular protocols in use today. Then the security issues and vulnerabilities associated with these protocols are examined.

With the criticality of SCADA system security established, the chapters that follow explore SCADA system vulnerabilities, risk issues, attacks, and attack routes, and they provide detailed guidance on countermeasures and other mechanisms that can be applied to effectively secure SCADA systems. In addition, related information, security standards, and reference documents are discussed. These publications provide extremely useful information for securing SCADA systems from cyberattacks.

The book concludes with an examination of the economics of implementing SCADA system security, organizational culture issues, perceptions (and misperceptions) of SCADA vulnerability, and current state of SCADA system security. This last topic is addressed in detail by examining SCADA security issues in the oil and gas industry, rail systems, and seaports. Finally, current advanced development programs, additional countermeasures, and legislation targeted to increase the effectiveness of SCADA security in the present and future are described.

What Is a SCADA System?

Supervisory control and data acquisition (SCADA) systems are vital components of most nations' critical infrastructures. They control pipelines, water and transportation systems, utilities, refineries, chemical plants, and a wide variety of manufacturing operations.

SCADA provides management with real-time data on production operations, implements more efficient control paradigms, improves plant and personnel safety, and reduces costs of operation. These benefits are made possible by the use of standard hardware and software in SCADA systems combined with improved communication protocols and increased connectivity to outside networks, including the Internet. However, these benefits are acquired at the price of increased vulnerability to attacks or erroneous actions from a variety of external and internal sources.

This chapter explores the evolution of SCADA systems, their characteristics, functions, typical applications, and general security issues.

History of Critical Infrastructure Directives

In 1996, Presidential Executive Order 13010 established the President's Commission on Critical Infrastructure Protection (PCCIP) to explore means to address the vulnerabilities in the U.S. critical infrastructure. Internet-based attacks and physical attacks were two of the major concerns that were to be considered by the committee. As a result of the committee's efforts, the FBI National Infrastructure Protection Center (NIPC) and the Critical Infrastructure Assurance Office (CIAO) were established in May 1998 by Presidential Decision Directive 63 (PDD 63). The main function of the NIPC was to conduct investigations relating to attacks against the critical infrastructure and issue associated warnings, when appropriate. The CIAO was designated as the main entity for managing the U.S. critical infrastructure protection (CIP) efforts, including coordinating the efforts of the different commercial and industrial entities affected.

As a consequence of the CIAO activities, the Communications and Information Sector Working Group (CISWG) was established with the mission to "promote information sharing and coordinated action to mitigate CIP risk and vulnerabilities in all levels of the Information and Communications (I&C) Sector." In addition, companies in eight critical industry sectors established a related entity, the Partnership for Critical Infrastructure Security (PCIS). The PCIS was formed to mitigate the vulnerabilities caused by the interdependence of many commercial and industrial organizations.

In response to the September 11, 2001 attacks, the president, on October 8, 2001, established the President's Critical Infrastructure Board (PCIB), the Office of Homeland Security, and the Homeland Security Council with Executive Order 13228. Also in October 2001, the USA Patriot Act was passed to provide U.S. government law enforcement agencies with increased authority to perform searches, monitor Internet communications, and conduct investigations.

On the economic front, in February 2003, President George W. Bush appointed the 30-member National Infrastructure Advisory Council (NIAC) from the private sector, state and local governments, and academia. NIAC's charter is to advise the president on information system security issues related to the various U.S. business sectors. Around the same time, President Bush issued Executive Order 1327, which discontinued the PCIB. This action was necessary because the functions of the PCIB were assumed by the Department of Homeland Security.

President Bush, in December 2003, announced Homeland Security Presidential Directives HSPD-7 and HSPD-8. HSPD-7 is a modification of PDD 63 that delineates the national policy and responsibilities of the executive departments, government corporations as defined by 5 U.S.C. 103(1), and the United States Postal Service relating to protection of the critical infrastructure. These are the executive departments:

- The Department of Homeland Security
- The Department of State
- The Department of the Treasury
- The Department of Defense
- The Department of Justice
- The Department of the Interior
- The Department of Agriculture
- The Department of Commerce
- The Department of Labor
- The Department of Housing and Urban Development
- The Department of Transportation
- The Department of Energy
- The Department of Education
- The Department of Veterans Affairs

HSPD-8 focuses on preparedness to prevent and respond to domestic terror attacks, disasters, and emergencies.

Figure 1-1 illustrates the timeline of the major activities relating to CIP in the United States.

SCADA System Evolution, Definitions, and Basic Architecture

Supervisory control and data acquisition (SCADA) means different things to different people, depending on their backgrounds and perspectives. Therefore, it is important to review the evolution of SCADA and its definition as understood by professionals and practitioners in the field.

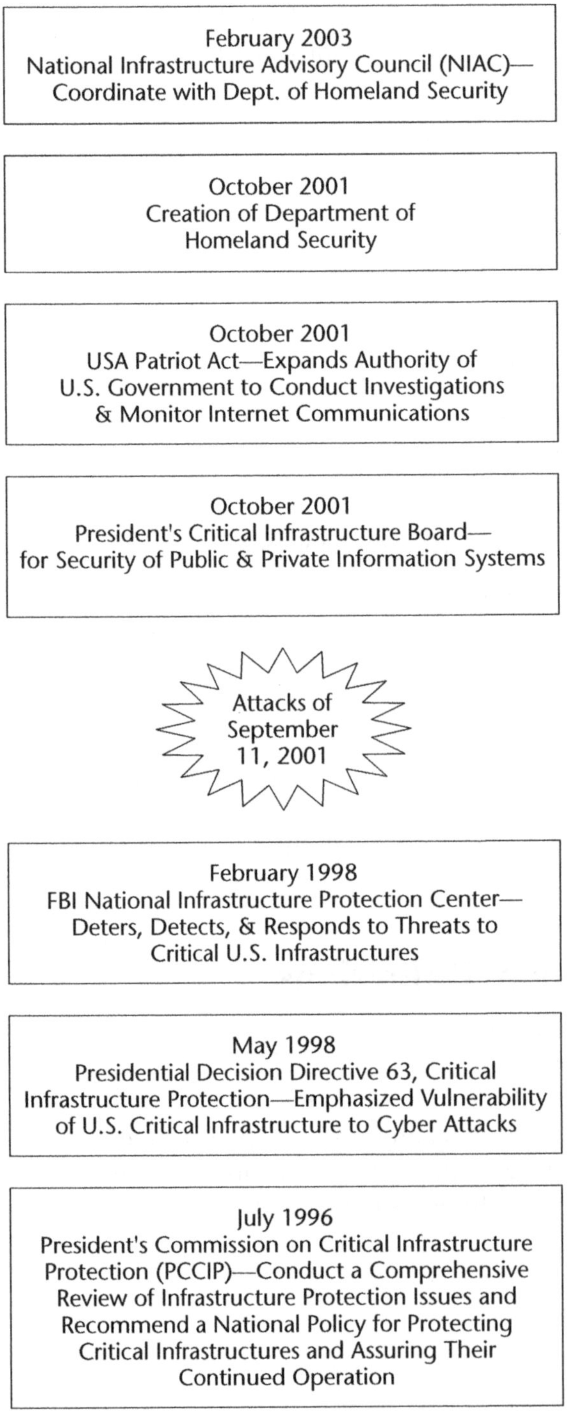

February 2003
National Infrastructure Advisory Council (NIAC)—
Coordinate with Dept. of Homeland Security

October 2001
Creation of Department of
Homeland Security

October 2001
USA Patriot Act—Expands Authority of
U.S. Government to Conduct Investigations
& Monitor Internet Communications

October 2001
President's Critical Infrastructure Board—
for Security of Public & Private Information Systems

Attacks of
September
11, 2001

February 1998
FBI National Infrastructure Protection Center—
Deters, Detects, & Responds to Threats to
Critical U.S. Infrastructures

May 1998
Presidential Decision Directive 63, Critical
Infrastructure Protection—Emphasized Vulnerability
of U.S. Critical Infrastructure to Cyber Attacks

July 1996
President's Commission on Critical Infrastructure
Protection (PCCIP)—Conduct a Comprehensive
Review of Infrastructure Protection Issues and
Recommend a National Policy for Protecting
Critical Infrastructures and Assuring Their
Continued Operation

Figure 1-1   Timeline of U.S. critical infrastructure protection activities

SCADA Evolution

The scope of SCADA has evolved from its beginnings in the 1960s. The advent of low-cost minicomputers such as the Digital Equipment Corporation PDP-8 and PDP-11 made computer control of process and manufacturing operations feasible. Programmable logic controllers (PLCs) progressed simultaneously. These latter devices implemented traditional *relay ladder logic* to control industrial processes. PLCs appealed to traditional control engineers who were accustomed to programming relay logic and who did not want to learn programming languages and operating systems. When microcomputers were developed, they were programmed and packaged to emulate PLCs in function, programming, and operation. In fact, competition developed between the two approaches and continues to this day.

Initially, control systems were confined to a particular plant. The associated control devices were local to the plant and not connected to an external network. The early control systems consisted of a central minicomputer or PLC that communicated with local controllers that interfaced with motors, pumps, valves, switches, sensors, and so on. Figure 1-2 illustrates this architecture.

This architecture is sometimes referred to as a *distributed control system.* Such systems are generally confined to locations close to each other, normally use a high-speed local network, and usually involve closed loop control. As a necessary requirement for the operation of these systems, companies and vendors developed their own communication protocols, many of which were proprietary.

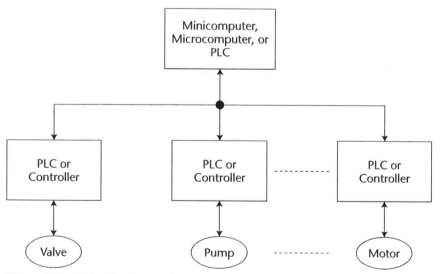

Figure 1-2   Typical local control system

As the technical capabilities of computers, operating systems, and networks improved, organizational management pushed for increased knowledge of the real-time status of remote plant operations. Also, in organizations with a number of geographically separated operations, remote data acquisition, control, and maintenance became increasingly attractive from management and cost standpoints. These capabilities are known collectively as *supervisory control and data acquisition* or SCADA.

SCADA Definition

Listed here are two typical definitions of a SCADA system and the source of each definition:

- SCADA is the technology that enables a user to collect data from one or more distant facilities and/or send limited control instructions to those facilities. *SCADA: Supervisory Control and Data Acquisition* by Stuart A. Boyer, published by ISA The Instrumentation, Systems, and Automation Society; 3rd edition.

- A system operating with coded signals over communication channels so as to provide control of RTU (Remote Terminal Unit) equipment. *IEEE Standard C37.1-1994, Definition, Specification, and Analysis of Systems Used for Supervisory Control, Data Acquisition, and Automatic Control.* (The RTU is discussed in the next section.)

Additional definitions associated with SCADA systems are given in Table 1-1. This listing is not meant to be all-inclusive, but describes some important terms used in the application of SCADA systems.

Table 1-1 SCADA-Related Definitions

TERM	DEFINITION
deterministic	Degree to which an activity can be performed within a predictable timeframe.
DeviceNet	An Allen Bradley control network protocol that is used to connect PLCs and local controllers.
ControlNet	An Allen Bradley communications protocol applied to control systems.
Data Highway, Data Highway +	Allen Bradley communications protocols.
fieldbus	Communication protocols that facilitate interchange of messages among field devices. Some examples of fieldbus protocols are Foundation Fieldbus, Modbus, DeviceNet, and Profibus.

Table 1-1   *(continued)*

TERM	DEFINITION
hot stand-by system	A duplicate system that is kept in synchronism with the main system and that can assume control if the main system goes down.
proportional, integral, derivative (PID) control	Method used to calculate control parameters to maintain a predetermined set point. Mathematical techniques are used to calculate rates of change, time delays, and other functions necessary to determine the corrections to be applied.
real-time (adjective)	An action that occurs at the same rate as actual time; no lag time, no processing time.
real-time operating system (RTOS)	A computer operating system that implements process and services in a deterministic manner.

SCADA System Architecture

Specific terminology is associated with the components of SCADA systems. These SCADA elements are defined as follows:

- **Operator:** Human operator who monitors the SCADA system and performs supervisory control functions for the remote plant operations.

- **Human machine interface (HMI):** Presents data to the operator and provides for control inputs in a variety of formats, including graphics, schematics, windows, pull-down menus, touch-screens, and so on.

- **Master terminal unit (MTU):** Equivalent to a master unit in a master/slave architecture. The MTU presents data to the operator through the HMI, gathers data from the distant site, and transmits control signals to the remote site. The transmission rate of data between the MTU and the remote site is relatively low and the control method is usually open loop because of possible time delays or data flow interruptions.

- **Communications means:** Communication method between the MTU and remote controllers. Communication can be through the Internet, wireless or wired networks, or the switched public telephone network.

- **Remote terminal unit (RTU):** Functions as a slave in the master/slave architecture. Sends control signals to the device under control, acquires data from these devices, and transmits the data to the MTU. An RTU may be a PLC. The data rate between the RTU and controlled device is relatively high and the control method is usually closed loop.

A general diagram of a SCADA system is shown in Figure 1-3.

Modern SCADA architectures rely heavily on standard protocols and digital data transmission. For example, a communications protocol such as the Foundation Fieldbus, which is discussed in Chapter 3, is applied in conjunction with industrial Ethernet radios. These Ethernet radios provide data rates of 512 Kbps, a large increase over those provided by EIA-232 serial links. For security, industrial Ethernet access points use spread-spectrum frequency hopping technology with encryption.

As discussed previously, a SCADA architecture comprises two levels: a master or client level at the supervisory control center and a slave or data server level that interacts with the processes under control. In addition to the hardware, the software components of the SCADA architecture are important. Here are some of the typical SCADA software components:

- SCADA master/client
    - Human machine interface
    - Alarm handling
    - Event and log monitoring
    - Special applications
    - ActiveX or Java controls
- SCADA slave/data server
    - Real-time system manager
    - Data processing applications
    - Report generator
    - Alarm handling
    - Drivers and interfaces to control components
    - Spreadsheet
    - Data logging
    - Archiving
    - Charting and trending

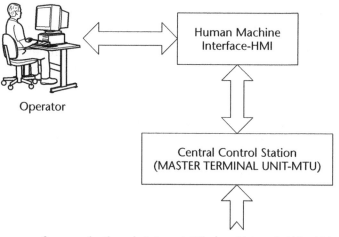

Operator

Human Machine
Interface-HMI

Central Control Station
(MASTER TERMINAL UNIT-MTU)

Communication via Internet, Wireless Network, Wired Network, or Switched
Public Telephone Network
(Relatively low data rate, usually open loop control)

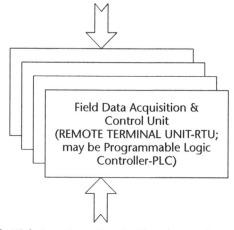

Field Data Acquisition &
Control Unit
(REMOTE TERMINAL UNIT-RTU;
may be Programmable Logic
Controller-PLC)

(Relatively High Data Rate, Usually Closed Loop Control)

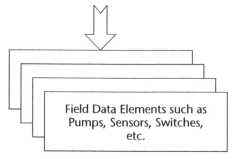

Field Data Elements such as
Pumps, Sensors, Switches,
etc.

Figure 1-3   Typical SCADA system architecture

SCADA Applications

SCADA is pervasive throughout the world. As discussed previously, it permeates the world's critical infrastructures, monitoring and controlling a variety of processes and operations. Examples of common SCADA systems are shown in Figures 1-4 through 1-8 to illustrate the diversity of their application domains. However, it is useful to note the similarities in their architectures.

In some of the examples, the EIA-232 and EIA-485 standards are used. EIA-232, formerly known as RS-232, was developed in the 1960s by the Electronic Industries Association (EIA) as a data communications standard. EIA-232 addresses serial data links and specifies the data exchange protocol, signal voltages and timing, signal functions, and the mechanical connectors to be used. EIA-232 signals are asynchronous with typical data rates of 20 Kbps.

EIA-485 is also an asynchronous serial data communications standard with typical data rates of 10 Mbps and the ability to transmit data over longer distance links than EIA-232. It was formerly known as RS-485.

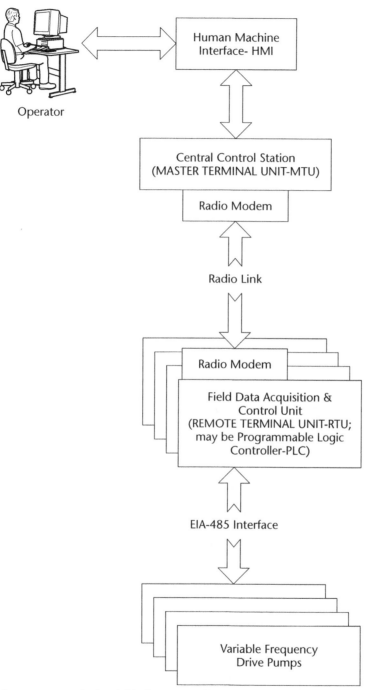

Figure 1-4   Typical variable frequency drive pump oil field SCADA system

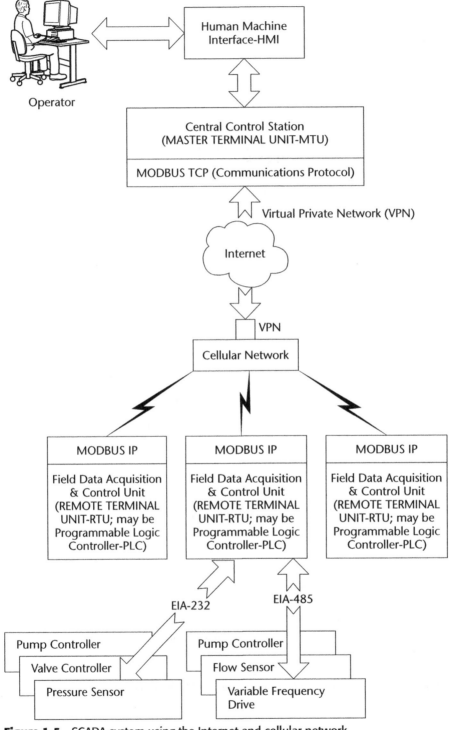

Figure 1-5   SCADA system using the Internet and cellular network

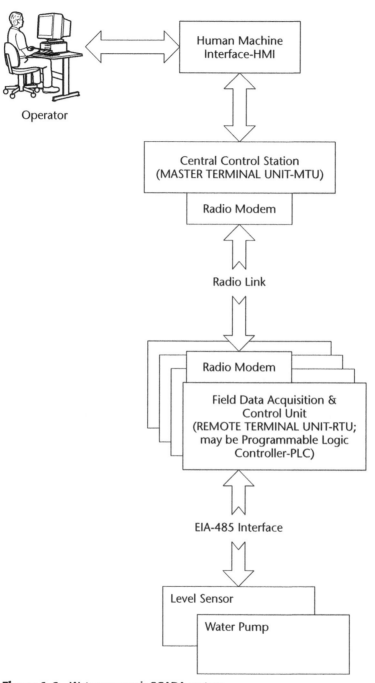

Figure 1-6 Water reservoir SCADA system

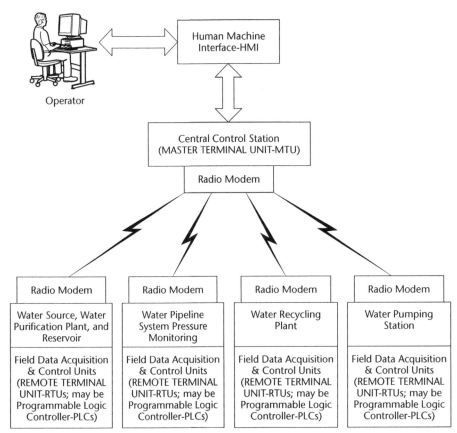

Figure 1-7   General SCADA water treatment facility

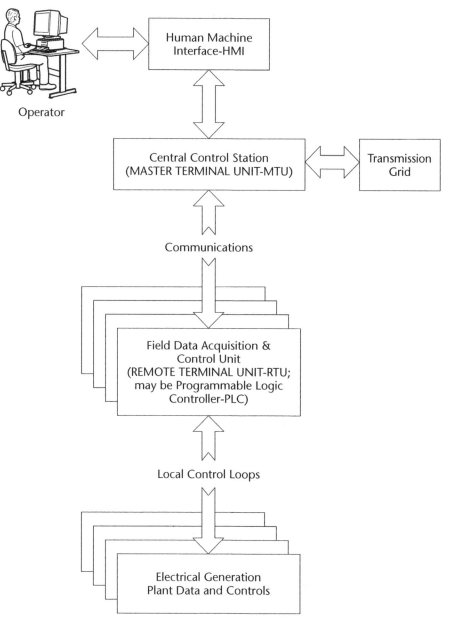

Figure 1-8   Electrical generating plant SCADA system

SCADA System Security Issues Overview

For reasons of efficiency, maintenance, and economics, data acquisition and control platforms have migrated from isolated in-plant networks using proprietary hardware and software to PC-based systems using standard software, network protocols, and the Internet. The downside of this transition has been to expose SCADA systems to the same vulnerabilities and threats that plague Windows-based PCs and their associated networks. Some typical attacks that might be mounted against SCADA systems that employ standard hardware and software are listed here:

- Malicious code such as viruses, Trojan horses, and worms
- Unauthorized disclosure of critical data
- Unauthorized modification and manipulation of critical data
- Denial of service
- Unauthorized access to audit logs and modification of audit logs

Most SCADA systems, particularly the local PLCs or controllers, have to operate in real-time or near real-time environments. Thus, they cannot afford delays that might be caused by information security software and that interfere with critical control decisions affecting personnel safety, product quality, and operating costs. Also, plant SCADA system components do not usually have excess memory capacity that can accommodate relatively large programs associated with security monitoring activities.

In summary, conventional information technology (IT) systems are concerned with providing for internal and external connectivity, productivity, extensive security mechanisms for authentication and authorization, and the three major information security principles of confidentiality, availability, and integrity. Conversely, SCADA systems emphasize reliability, real-time response, tolerance of emergency situations where passwords might be incorrectly entered, personnel safety, product quality, and plant safety.

SCADA and IT Convergence

There is an emerging trend in many organizations comprising SCADA and conventional IT units toward consolidating some overlapping activities. For example, control engineering might be absorbed or closely integrated with the corporate IT department. This trend is motivated by cost savings achieved by consolidating disparate platforms, networks, software, and maintenance tools. In addition, integrating SCADA data collection and monitoring with corporate financial and customer data provides management with an increased ability to run the organization more efficiently and effectively.

This integration, however, comes with some difficulty. Relative to information security for example, the security architectures of SCADA and corporate IT systems traditionally have focused on different priorities. With a merging of the two systems, both SCADA and corporate IT use the same security model. Issues such as modems connected to one system compromising the other, the possibility of the corporate Internet connection exposing the SCADA system, the real-time, deterministic requirements of SCADA systems, and the round-the-clock operation of SCADA systems require merging of the disparate cultures of SCADA and IT. A good example of this sort of problem is the routinely scheduled downtime for IT organizations to upgrade software, perform back-ups, and so on. Such downtime cannot be tolerated in most SCADA systems.

Conventional IT Security and Relevant SCADA Issues

Over the years, information system security professionals developed a number of generally accepted best practices to protect networks and computing infrastructures from malicious attacks. However, these practices cannot be applied directly to SCADA systems without accounting for the different requirements of IT and SCADA systems. The following list provides examples of IT best practices and the state of their application to SCADA systems:

Audit and monitoring logs: After-the-fact analysis of audit trails is a useful means to detect past events. Monitoring, on the other hand, implies real-time capture of data as a system is operating. Both techniques are successfully employed in IT systems. Their application to SCADA systems will yield benefits similar to those derived from their use in IT systems. Because of the varying ages and sophistication of some SCADA system components, many do not have logging capabilities. The cost of installing, operating, and maintaining extensive auditing and monitoring capabilities in a SCADA application must be weighed against the potential benefits.

Biometrics: Biometrics are attractive because they base authentication on a physical characteristic of the individual attempting to access relevant components of a SCADA system. Currently, biometrics are promising, but are not completely reliable. Depending on the characteristic being examined, there might be a high number of false rejections or false acceptances, throughput problems, human factor issues, and possible compromises of the system. However, the technology is progressing and biometrics should become a viable option for controlling SCADA system access.

Firewalls: Firewalls can be used to screen message traffic between a corporate IT network and a SCADA network. Thus, in many instances, a firewall can protect SCADA systems from penetrations that have occurred on the corporate side. Some issues that have to be considered when applying firewalls to SCADA systems are the delays introduced into data transmissions, the skill and overhead required set up and manage firewalls, and the lack of firewalls designed to interface with some popular SCADA protocols.

Intrusion detection systems: Intrusion detection systems (IDSs) are either host-based or network-based. A host-based IDS can detect attacks against the host system, but does not monitor the network. Alternatively, a network-based IDS views the network by monitoring network traffic and assesses the traffic for malicious intent. IDSs are useful in protecting SCADA systems, but cannot be universally applied because, at this time, IDSs are not available for some SCADA protocols. As with other safeguards, IDSs might slow down certain SCADA operations and their cost and operation have to be weighed against the potential benefits derived from their use.

Malicious code detection and elimination: The computational overhead associated with detecting and eliminating malicious code that might infect a SCADA system can seriously affect the real-time performance of SCADA system components. Activities such as running antivirus software, updating virus signature databases, and quarantining or deleting malicious code require time and computing cycles that might not be available on SCADA system components. Updating virus databases from the Internet also exposes the SCADA systems to additional viruses and attacks from the Internet. Again, the cost of antivirus implementations must be weighed against the perceived SCADA risks and benefits of such software.

Passwords: In a SCADA environment, a control operator might need to enter a password to gain access to a device in an emergency. If the operator types in the password incorrectly a few times, a conventional IT security paradigm, which presumes an intruder trying to guess the password, is to lock out the operator. Locking out the operator is not a good thing in real-time control environments. For operators on local control devices, passwords might be eliminated or made extremely simple. At the supervisory level, better and longer passwords might be used, two-factor authentication employed, and challenge-response tokens used. In situations where the passwords might be subject to interception when transmitted over networks, encryption should be considered to protect the password from compromise.

Public-key cryptography: With public-key or asymmetric-key cryptography, there is no need to exchange secret keys between sender and receiver. A public key is available to anyone wishing to communicate with the holder of the corresponding and mathematically related private key. The private key is protected and known only to the receiving party. The main feature of public-key cryptography is that it is virtually impossible to derive the private key from the known public key. Public-key cryptography also provides the ability for a sender to digitally sign a document and transmit it for anyone to read who can access the sender's public key. This signing guarantees that the document was sent by the owner of the private key of the public-key–private-key pair. As one can deduce, key management, including certification that the public key actually belongs to the named person, is an important issue that has to be handled by the organization. Relative to SCADA operations, public-key cryptosystems require relatively long processing times that are incompatible with the real-time requirements of control systems. Symmetric-key cryptosystems, discussed in the next section, are more suitable for use in the SCADA environment.

Symmetric-key cryptography: With symmetric-key cryptography, also known as secret-key cryptography, the sender and receiver have to share a common, secret key. This key is used to encrypt the message at the transmitting end and decrypt the message at the receiving end. Thus, the secret keys have to be distributed securely from all transmitters to all receivers. This distribution is a concern. One popular solution is to use public-key cryptography to distribute the secret key and then use symmetric-key cryptography to send the message. Because the key length is relatively short compared to the messages, time is not an issue with public-key cryptography. Symmetric-key cryptography is orders of magnitude faster in operation than public-key cryptography. Symmetric-key cryptography has not yet been widely applied to SCADA systems. It is applicable to data transmitted over a long-distance SCADA network and is not as important in local plant control loops. Symmetric key encryption will be applied to the critical portions of a SCADA network.

Role-based access control: This type of access control is gaining popularity in government and industry sectors because of its ability to accommodate changes in personnel and organizations. In this type of security control, access is based on the role of a person in an organization rather than the identity of the individual. It has not yet been widely applied to SCADA systems but holds promise for use at the supervisory level of SCADA operations.

Redundancy as a Component of SCADA Security

In addition to technical and administrative security controls, various physical security measures can be applied to protect SCADA systems.

Backup, duplicate, geographically separated control centers can provide redundancy and, therefore, protection against human attacks and natural disasters. On a smaller scale, a hot backup standby SCADA system at the supervisory control center provides a means to continue operating if the primary system is disabled. As an additional security layer, the SCADA control center could be located in a remote area in an unmarked, inconspicuous building.

SCADA System Desirable Properties

Figure 1-9 summarizes the general state of SCADA at this time. The figure depicts a typical SCADA system that incorporates standard hardware and software platforms, such as PCs and Windows. The SCADA system is linked to external networks, corporate IT operations, and remote, possibly insecure, access points such as modems. Because standard hardware and software are used, the equipment is vulnerable to the same attacks that historically have been mounted against PCs and Windows.

A successful, unauthorized penetration of a SCADA system could result in an intruder taking control of a master or slave unit, disrupting critical processes, falsifying data, and even initiating actions that could result in the loss of human life and destruction of the plant under control.

A good description of the desired properties of a SCADA system is given in the North American Electric Reliability Council (NERC) definition of SCADA reliability objectives. Even though the definition addresses the electric utility industry, the properties can be extrapolated to all components of a nation's critical infrastructure. NERC Form 715 defines reliability as:

- **Adequacy:** The capacity to meet system demand within major component ratings in the presence of scheduled and unscheduled outage of generation and transmission components or facilities
- **Security:** A system's capability to withstand system disturbances arising from faults and unscheduled removal of bulk power supply elements without further loss of facilities or cascading outages

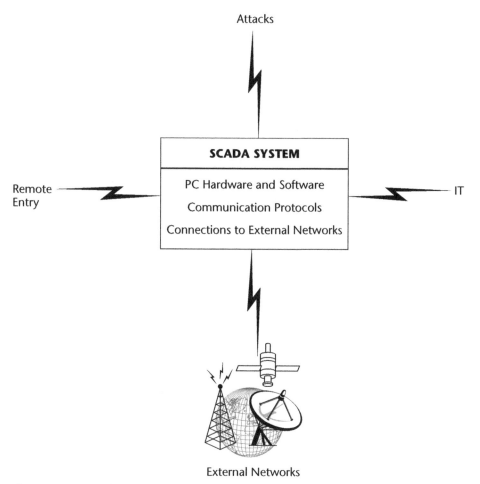

Figure 1-9 Typical SCADA System Links

If the NERC definitions of adequacy and security were modified to apply to SCADA systems in general, they might read as follows:

- **Adequacy:** The capacity to meet system operating specifications within major component ratings in the presence of scheduled and unscheduled outage of system components or facilities

- **Security:** A system's capability to withstand system disturbances arising from faults or unauthorized internal or external actions without further loss of facilities, compromise of human safety, and loss of production.

Summary

From 1996 to 2003, a number of Executive Orders and Presidential Decision Directives were issued to address the security of the U.S. critical infrastructure. A key security concern in the infrastructure is the vulnerability of SCADA systems.

As SCADA systems progressed from stand-alone architectures using proprietary hardware, software, and protocols to interconnected elements comprising PCs, Windows, and standard protocols, they also became more vulnerable to attacks. In addition, SCADA systems are being integrated into corporate IT systems, which have different security and reliability characteristics than the more stringent SCADA requirements.

A number of conventional IT security controls can be applied to SCADA systems if the specific needs of these systems are taken into account. Government, industrial organizations, and standards groups have identified the need for additional research and development into SCADA system security and are developing guidelines for protecting SCADA systems from cyberattacks.

CHAPTER 2

SCADA Systems in the Critical Infrastructure

Chapter 1 includes a brief overview of some typical SCADA applications. In this chapter, nine applications are discussed in more detail to highlight the vital role that SCADA plays in a nation's critical infrastructure. In order to emphasize the impact of a successful attack against SCADA systems employed in key applications, it is necessary to understand these operations.

Employment of SCADA Systems

SCADA systems are employed in a wide variety of processes and plants, ranging from supervising and controlling the production of necessary but toxic substances, to optimizing manufacturing lines. An analysis of these processes and production methods reveals the serious repercussions of a threat realized against the associated SCADA systems.

Petroleum Refining

Petroleum refineries are extremely important elements in a nation's critical infrastructure. Goods and services depend on transportation by planes, trucks, cars, trains, and boats and on the myriad of engines running on petroleum-based fuels.

To achieve economic viability, petroleum refineries have to operate at high volumes in a continuous process. Thus, they are built to handle large capacities and run on a 24-hour, 7-days-per-week basis. There are 146 petroleum refineries in the U.S. with capacities ranging from 50,000 barrels per day to approximately 600,000 barrels per day. Any material reduction of refining capacity can cause great harm to the U.S. economy.

For ease of receiving the raw crude oil and transporting the refinery products, most refineries are located near ports or rivers. In most instances, port functions and security are dependent, directly or indirectly, on the proper operation of SCADA systems. These systems control a variety of interdependent resources that are crucial to the safe and secure operation of the nation's ports. A terrorist attack on one or more ports that receive crude oil for refinery processing would have a catastrophic impact on U.S. oil production and the economy. As part of emergency procedures, many or all of the other operating ports would be shut down in anticipation of similar attacks. Some of the possible SCADA attack targets that would affect oil production include those controlling port energy, communications, water, bridges, dams, and pipelines.

Other SCADA attack targets are those involved in controlling the petroleum refining process. To better identify potential vulnerabilities, the following section reviews the basic petroleum refining steps.

The Basic Refining Process

The principal function of a refinery is to distill and perform various chemical reactions on the crude oil input. These operations require temperatures on the order of 500 to 1,000 degrees Fahrenheit and pressures ranging from 150 pounds per square inch (psi) to 3,500 psi. As part of the refining process, combustible and toxic substances are produced. In addition to the general fuel products, hydrogen (H) is used and generated and the toxic compounds hydrogen sulfide (H_2S) and ammonia (NH_3) are generated.

In a refinery distillation column, the component hydrocarbons can be separated because they have different boiling points that range from approximately 50 degrees Fahrenheit to 1,400 degrees Fahrenheit. This process is called fractionation, which is the result of adding heat to the bottom of the distillation tower and establishing a temperature profile through the tower from bottom to top. The proper temperature gradient is maintained by removing heat from the top of the tower. The lower boiling point hydrocarbons migrate to the top of the tower as vapors and the higher boiling point substances are found at the bottom of the tower in the liquid state. Hydrocarbons in the intermediate boiling point range are extracted from the side of the tower. These substances usually contain sulfur in amounts that exceed those tolerable in the finished product and that can contaminate catalysts used in the refining process.

The sulfur is removed through *hydrotreating*, which mixes hydrogen gas with the hydrocarbon stream at high temperatures and uses a catalyst to support the desired chemical reaction. This operation is known as *hydrodesulfurization* or (HDS). A product of this reaction is the toxic gas hydrogen sulfide (H_2S), which results from hydrogen atoms combing with sulfur atoms. A similar process uses hydrogen to remove unwanted nitrogen from hydrocarbon streams. This process is known as hydrodenitrogenation (HDN) and yields ammonia, NH_3, as a product of the reaction.

In another process, alkylates are produced as blending agents for higher-octane gasolines. The alkylation process requires catalysis in an environment of either highly corrosive hydrofluoric or sulfuric acid. Hydrofluoric acid exists in a vapor form and, unless properly contained, can escape and cause serious harm to personnel and the environment.

A general block diagram depicting the petroleum refining process and resultant products is shown in Figure 2-1.

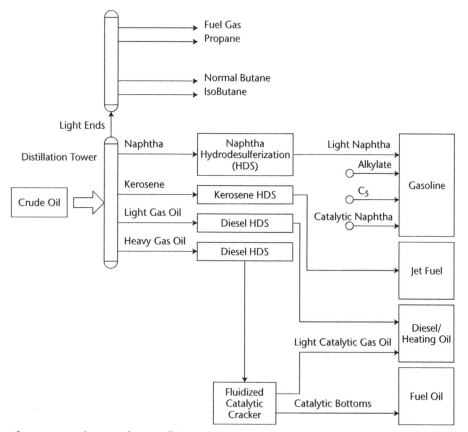

Figure 2-1 The petroleum refining process

Possible Attack Consequences

It is clear that petroleum refineries must be kept under strict control in all phases of hydrocarbon processing or serious damage to human life, property, and, eventually, the economy will result. With refineries under SCADA control, they are, by definition, connected to wide area networks and use protocols that are subject to threats and attacks that can seize or impair control of critical refinery processes. Results of successful SCADA system attacks might include exceeding temperature and pressure limits, interruption of the process flow, escape of toxic liquids and vapors, and contamination of catalysts. These conditions can produce a variety of harmful events ranging from defective products to fires, explosions, incapacitation of the refinery, human injury or death, and contamination of wide areas.

Unfortunately, the consequences of incorrect procedures or improper control of a refinery were illustrated in a number of incidents in Texas. In April of 1947, ammonium nitrate stored in two ships docked at a port near a Texas City, Texas, refinery exploded and destroyed much of the city. Because of that explosion, 576 people died. In the same city, on March 31, 2004, a number of explosions erupted in the BP refinery, severely damaging the plant, but with no reported loss of life. More recently, on March 23, 2005, an explosion occurred in a chemical unit at the same BP refinery in Texas City, injuring over 100 people and killing 15. (The BP refinery covers approximately 1,200 acres of land and processes 433,000 barrels of crude oil per day. This amount is 3 percent of the U.S. crude oil processing capacity.)

The explosion was located in a refinery unit that increases the octane of gasoline. This explosion occurred when the plant was being returned to production after annual maintenance. Experts note that most explosions occur at this time, when the processes have not yet stabilized.

Nuclear Power Generation

Another component of the U.S. critical infrastructure that is sensitive to SCADA attacks is the nuclear power plant. In a nuclear power plant, the nuclear reactor generates heat that produces high-pressure steam. The steam is used to power turbines that provide rotational energy to electrical generators. The process is similar to that used in fossil fuel plants, but the source of heat in a nuclear power plant is the reactor instead of the burning of fossil fuels.

The heat is the result of a nuclear fission reaction in which atoms with large atomic numbers are broken into two atoms by collisions with neutrons. This *splitting* also produces a relatively large amount of energy and releases additional neutrons. The newly generated neutrons, in turn, collide with other large atomic number atoms and a chain reaction is sustained. A typical reaction is the breakdown of Uranium 235 (U-235), which creates strontium, xenon, an average of 2.47 neutrons, and 203 million electron-volts (MEV) of energy. Here is a simplified expression describing this breakdown:

U-235 + neutron ⇨ Xe-139 + Sr-95 + 2.47 neutrons + 203 MEV

In order to sustain the reaction, *fast* neutrons that are generated must be slowed down to energy levels that are optimum for colliding with the U-235 atoms. These slower neutrons are known as *thermal* neutrons. To accomplish this task, a *moderator* is put in the core. A widely used moderator that also performs heat transfer is water. The energy released by this sustained chain reaction is manifested as heat that generates steam to power the steam turbines. Control of the nuclear reactor is accomplished by moving neutron-absorbing materials in the form of rods in and out of the reactor. A typical rod is composed of silver, indium, and cadmium.

In the United States, the nuclear power plants use water as a moderator and coolant. These reactors are known as *light water* reactors. The two main types of light water reactors are defined by the state of the water. In the *boiling water reactor* (BWR), the water is allowed to boil. The result is steam that is used to directly power the turbines. This steam exhibits a low level of radioactivity with a half-life of about one-half second. In *the pressurized water reactor* (PWR), two separate loops are used with a heat exchanger to isolate the low radioactivity steam from the reactor from the steam circulated to the turbines.

The Boiling Water Reactor

A typical BWR that generates 1,220 megawatts of electrical power has approximately 180 neutron-absorbing control rods that have to be operated. Safety features for these reactors include an emergency core cooling system to prevent the core overheating. A general diagram of a boiling water reactor is given in Figure 2-2.

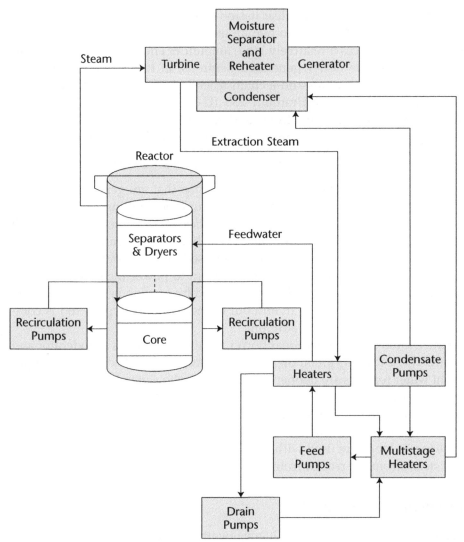

Figure 2-2 Boiling water reactor diagram

The Pressurized Water Reactor

The PWR is used widely throughout the world and in nuclear submarines. In this reactor, the coolant is kept under pressure to prevent boiling. It uses two separate steam loops as shown in Figure 2-3. The pressures in both loops, the primary and secondary, must be controlled for safe and proper operation. The critical pressure in the primary loop is controlled by a pressurizer inserted at the output of the reactor.

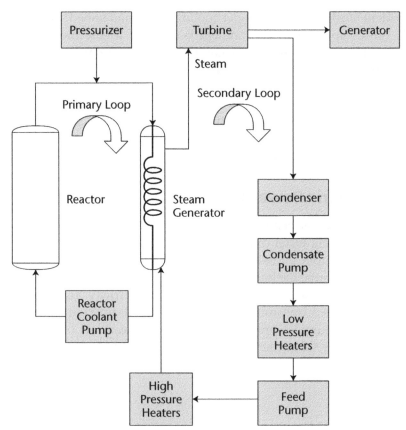

Figure 2-3   Pressurized water reactor

Possible Attack Consequences

As opposed to conventional fossil fuel, which can be completely shut off, the fuel for a nuclear power plant is installed and operates for one to two years. The chain reaction rate of a nuclear power plant has to be controlled over a variety of conditions and before and after refueling takes place. Furthermore, even when a nuclear plant is shut down, radioactive decay still takes place and heat is generated. This heat must be removed or the reactor core will melt, causing a situation similar to the accident at the Three Mile Island Unit 2 (TMI-2) nuclear power plant near Middletown, Pennsylvania, on March 28, 1979. In this incident, a partial meltdown of the reactor core was caused by a series of events including operator errors and malfunctioning equipment. Fortunately, only a small amount of radiation was released and there were no casualties. Because of this accident, the U.S. Nuclear Regulatory Commission (NRC) increased safety and oversight requirements for nuclear power plants.

The TMI incident illustrates that if proper cooling is not maintained, radioactive materials can escape to the environment because of a core meltdown. SCADA-type systems are responsible for controlling heat removal and handling other normal and emergency situations in the nuclear power plant. Therefore, any interference with the operation of the SCADA system can have dramatic and dangerous consequences.

Another issue is spent nuclear fuel, which also contains the radioactive products of the fission process. This spent fuel can be reprocessed to produce new fuel rods or it can be stored in pools in nuclear power plants.

Conventional Electric Power Generation

A conventional electric power generating facility produces electricity by harnessing the energy of falling water or by generating heat through the burning of fossil fuels. In this example, a fossil fuel plant is examined.

As in nuclear power plants, the heat is applied to water, steam is generated, and the steam is used to power turbines that turn electricity generators. The electrical energy is then transmitted and distributed at different voltages to power substations. Figure 2-4 provides a geographic overview of a fossil fuel electric plant and the subsequent path of the generated electricity to an end user.

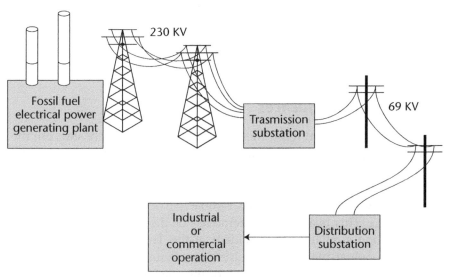

Figure 2-4   Electrical power generation and geographic distribution overview

In a coal-fired plant, the coal is crushed, stored in silos, pulverized, and conveyed into a furnace. The burning coal generates heat that impinges on a boiler and generates steam that is used to drive steam turbines. The turbines, in turn, drive electricity generators that provide power to the transmission and distribution grid. The steam is condensed and recirculated into the boiler to repeat the process. A local control room that is part of a SCADA system operates the plant and its processes. Figure 2-5 illustrates this process and the associated components.

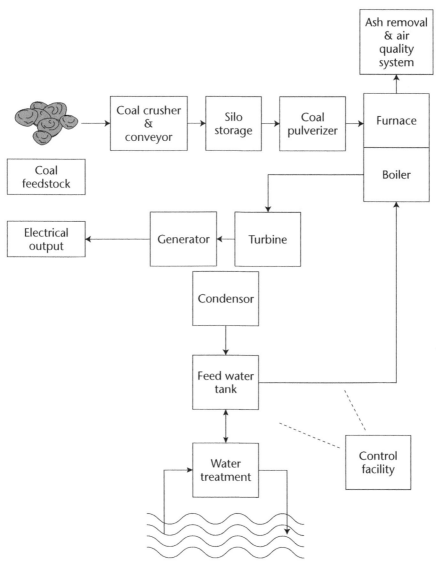

Figure 2-5 Typical fossil fuel power plant

There are many parameters and devices that have to be controlled for proper operation of the plant, including those related to emergencies. The main SCADA components are in the control room and at the substations. The local control remote terminal units (RTUs) are located throughout the plant at the needed control points. The control components include the following:

- Energy management computers
- Master supervisory PLC
- Master PLC hot backup
- Turbine control PLC
- Burner control PLC
- Air quality control PLC
- Water treatment PLC
- Boiler control PLC
- Conveyor system PLC
- Power substation local control PLCs

These control stations and their interactions are shown in Figure 2-6.

Petroleum Wellhead Pump Control

In unmanned petroleum production platforms, four to six oil producers can be connected to the production header. These clusters are controlled by a master wellhead hydraulic control panel that is connected to a SCADA system for remote control and monitoring. Actuators and valves that control the production well pressures are powered by electrical or pneumatic pumps. The SCADA system also monitors the wells for emergencies. Interference with the wellhead controls can result in blowouts, fires, damage to lives and equipment, destruction of oil reservoirs, and environmental damage. A typical wellhead pump control system is given in Figure 2-7.

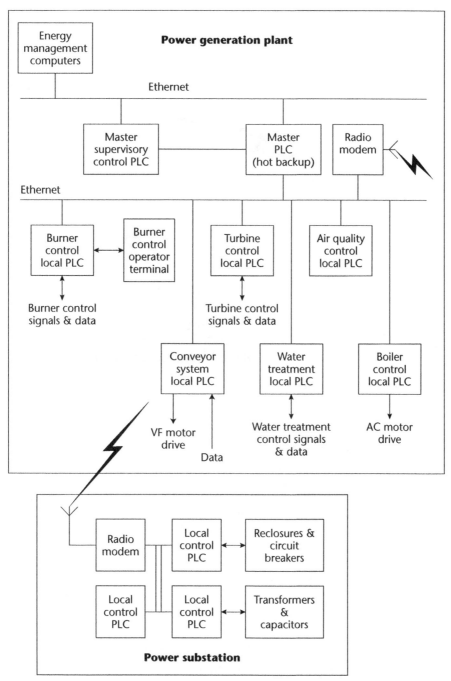

Figure 2-6   Plant control components

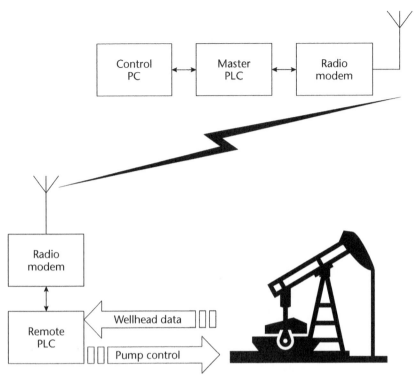

Figure 2-7   Wellhead pump control system

Water Purification System

In a typical water purification operation, water is pumped from a reservoir or other water source to a water purification plant. After purification, the water is pumped through a transmission system to the water consumers.

In designing a water purification system, the following items are considered:

- Future expandability
- Terrain traversed by the water pipelines
- Control of system functions and performance
- Maintenance of water quality

For this type of operation, a SCADA system is applied to control and monitor the water purification process, pumping systems, and pipeline pressures. Because of the distances involved in some installations, radio modems are used to communicate between the central supervisory station and the remote locations. Figure 2-8 depicts a SCADA system for a typical water purification plant.

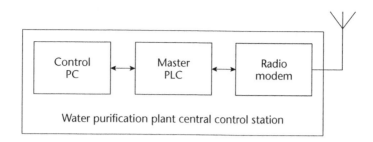

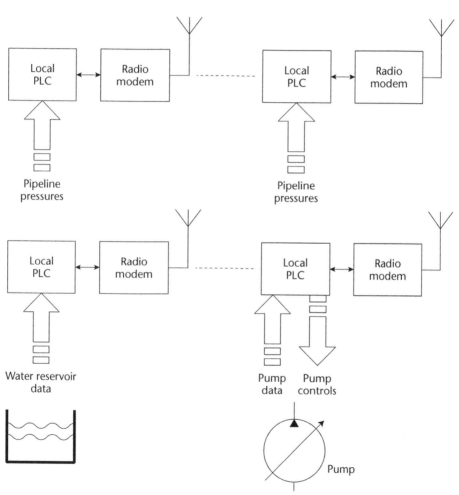

Figure 2-8   Water purification and transmission system

Possible attack scenarios on a water purification and transmission system include jamming or interference with radio communication links, disabling or interrupting the water purification process, inserting false pressure and pump data to disrupt transmission operations, and modifying water reservoir information.

Crane Control

Even though crane control does not seem to be a critical link in the nation's infrastructure, cranes and related mobile equipment are widely used in factories and different types of plants across the United States. Therefore, it is useful to examine their associated control mechanisms. In Figure 2-9, an overhead crane is controlled by a local PLC with control signals transmitted over a radio modem from a supervisory control station. A typical radio modem uses spread spectrum communications operating in the 902–928 MHz industrial, scientific, and medical (ISM) band, which does not require an FCC license.

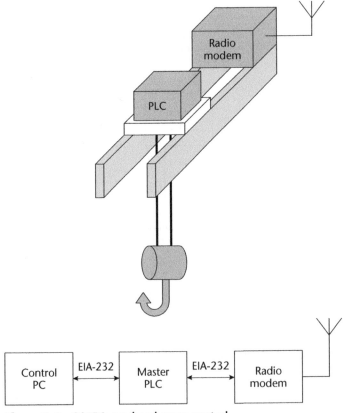

Figure 2-9   SCADA overhead crane control

Successful attacks on the control PC or on the local PLC at the crane can result in its crashing into limits on the rails, dropping large and sometimes extremely sensitive loads, and harming humans and equipment.

SCADA in the Corporation

As discussed in Chapter 1, there is a trend toward integrating SCADA systems with corporate IT systems. The reasons for this integration include the following:

- Consolidating overlapping activities
- Cost savings in standardization of platforms, networks, software, and maintenance tools
- Integrating corporate financial and customer data with SCADA data collection and monitoring
- Providing management with comprehensive data to make critical decisions

Relative to security, the integration of SCADA and corporate systems opens a window of vulnerability between them. Internet connections and modems provide possible attack routes to both systems.

Figure 2-10 illustrates a corporate architecture using a SCADA system.

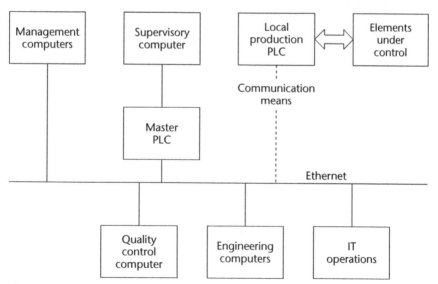

Figure 2-10   View of corporate IT architecture using SCADA

In Figure 2-10, enterprise computers including those in management, engineering, quality control, and IT departments are logically and, many times, physically, on the same Ethernet bus as SCADA supervisory computers that are communicating with remote RTUs.

Consolidation provides efficiency at the expense of possible large-scale intrusions and the resulting damage that can be caused through the exploitation of the corporation's vulnerabilities.

Chemical Plant

There are approximately 15,000 locations in the United States that either store or manufacture toxic chemicals. Of this number, about 100 are chemical plants. Many of these facilities are close to cities and residential neighborhoods, where they pose a threat to health, life, and property in the event of a terrorist attack or operational malfunction. It is estimated that an accident or sabotage at one of these facilities can kill, displace, or injure more than eight million people. These plants or storage facilities manufacture or hold highly toxic chemicals such as chlorine gas, benzene, anhydrous ammonia, and boron trifluoride. The latter is colorless gas that can kill by attacking a person's mucous membranes.

Benzene Production

As an example, the production of benzene (C_6H_6) is reviewed to highlight the chemicals involved in the production process and the effects of interfering with SCADA system operations.

Benzene is produced by three different methods. These methods are steam cracking, catalytic reforming, and toluene hydrodealkylation. This example features toluene hydrodealkylation.

In the toluene hydrodealkylation process, hydrogen reacts with toluene over a catalyst bed with temperatures between 500 and 600 degrees Celsius and 40 to 60 atmospheres of pressure. Here is the chemical reaction:

$$C_7H_8 + H_2 \Rightarrow C_6H_6 + CH_4$$

Figure 2-11 is a process flow diagram for benzene production.

The major hazards involved with disruption or hijacking of SCADA control of a benzene production facility are associated with the handling and reaction of the constituent components and resulting products. These items include toluene, hydrogen, benzene, and methane.

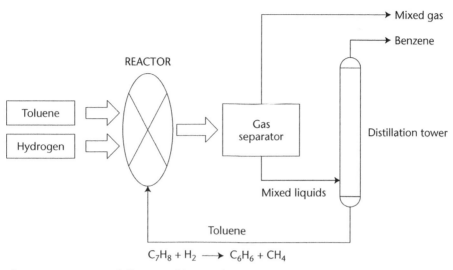

Figure 2-11   General diagram of benzene production plant

Toluene (C_7H_8) is flammable in liquid and vapor form. It is a colorless liquid with a density greater than air. Thus, it can spread over wide areas and cause great damage if ignited. It has a density less than water, so that it remains at the surface and, again, can spread over large distances. Toluene can accumulate a static charge when flowing or shaken, thus increasing the possible chance of ignition. When heated, toluene forms toxic gases, which can cause drowsiness, dizziness, nausea, and headaches when inhaled. Toluene stored in closed containers can explode when heated by an external source, such as a fire.

Hydrogen is flammable and, if released and combined with an oxidizer, can result in a fire and explosion. When hydrogen is converted from a liquid to a gas, it generates an overpressure that can rupture containers, cause ignition, and produce dangerous fragments from the broken containers. The overpressure from a hydrogen explosion and contact with a hydrogen fire can cause serious harm to personnel and equipment.

Methane (CH_4) is a product of the benzene process. It is a combustible, colorless, odorless gas with a density lighter than air at room temperature. Methane mixtures of approximately 10 percent in air can cause explosions; breathing methane causes asphyxiation when inhaled by displacing oxygen in the lungs.

Benzene (C_6H_6) can cause drowsiness, dizziness, and even death when inhaled. Benzene is classified by the U.S. Department of Health and Human Services as a carcinogen; exposure can also affect the blood and immune system.

Embedded Systems

Many RTU-type devices are embedded systems, comprising processor modules, analog and digital inputs and outputs, and communication ports such as EIA-232 and 485 interfaces. Thus, an *embedded system* is defined as a combination of computer hardware, software, and other components designed to perform a specific function.

Embedded systems used in industrial applications are designed to operate in temperature extremes and noisy environments, and they are resistant to rough handling.

These RTUs are designed for applications in a variety of venues, including outside for rail system monitoring, and in oil refineries, steel plants, or electrical substations. They are employed in the conventional SCADA architecture, but are modular devices designed for ease of deployment and maintenance.

Exploitation of SCADA systems can involve gaining control of RTUs or modifying data transmitted to and from RTUs managing sensitive processes.

Why We Should Worry about These Operations

As this chapter illustrates, compromised SCADA systems have the potential for inflicting significant damage to human life and critical infrastructure. In many places, such as in chemical plants and refineries, vulnerabilities to physical and SCADA attacks still exist, and the same is true of ports, pipelines, electrical utilities, and water treatment plants.

As with most situations, there are both positive and negative aspects regarding the state of SCADA system protection. The positive side is that the SCADA constituency is becoming increasingly aware of their systems' vulnerabilities and is taking action through increased emphasis on information system security peculiar to the needs of SCADA users. In addition, standards organizations concerned with data acquisition and control are developing guidelines and standards for the security of SCADA systems. National laboratories have established SCADA test beds to evaluate the most effective security measures. Organizations such as the National Institute of Standards and Technology (NIST) have initiated programs focusing on SCADA security.

The negative side is that these standards, guidelines, and security measures have not been universally applied to critical infrastructure applications because of lack of funds, management apathy, other issues perceived as higher priority, and lack of guidance in some sectors.

In Chapter 6, the emerging standards are discussed in detail, but an overview of some of the important ones along with related initiatives is presented here to demonstrate the attention that the protection of SCADA systems is receiving. These efforts include the following:

- The Instrumentation, Systems, and Automation Society (ISA) document ISA-TR99.00.01-2004, *Security Technologies for Manufacturing and Control Systems*, March 11, 2004: This report evaluates a number of electronic security tools and methods for use in manufacturing and control systems.

- ISA Technical Report ISA-TR99.00.02-2004, *Integrating Electronic Security into the Manufacturing and Control System Environment*, April 2004: This report provides direction to appliers of control systems and security practitioners on achieving effective electronic security for these systems.

- The IEEE P1547 Series of Standards for Interconnection of Distributed Resources (DR) with Electric Power Systems (EPS): This series defines unifying standards for performance, operation, safety, and maintenance of interconnections of DR with EPS. The Sandia National Laboratories is focusing on a standards-based solution to the security of SCADA systems through the IEEE P1547 committees as well as the IEC TC 57 Working Groups.

- National SCADA Test Bed (NSTB): The NSTB is designed to test the vulnerabilities of control systems and related security software and hardware. It is run jointly by Sandia Laboratories and the Idaho National Engineering and Environmental Laboratories.

Summary

The security posture of SCADA systems is crucial to the security and safety of the nation's critical infrastructure. There is potential for great harm to human life and the national economy if SCADA systems are breached. Threats realized to SCADA systems can cause havoc in ports, chemical plants, power grids, refineries, and other critical activities. The efforts of industry and standards groups are targeted at reducing the vulnerabilities of these operations. However, at this time, these vulnerabilities remain in many crucial U.S. manufacturing and process resources.

The Evolution of SCADA Protocols

In order for two or more entities to communicate, they must speak the same language (protocol) and adhere to certain rules for initiating, conducting, and ending the communication. This chapter reviews the most popular protocols for communicating information over networks such as the Internet and explores proprietary and open protocols designed specifically for use in SCADA systems.

Evolution of SCADA Protocols

SCADA protocols evolved out of the need to send and receive data and control information locally and over distances in deterministic time. *Deterministic* in this context refers to the ability to predict the amount of time required for a transaction to take place when all relevant factors are known and understood. To accomplish communication in deterministic time for applications in refineries, electric utilities, and other users of SCADA systems, manufacturers of control devices, such as PLCs, developed their own protocols and communication bus structures. Table 3-1 summarizes some of these manufacturers and their corresponding protocols.

Table 3-1   SCADA Protocols

MANUFACTURER	PROTOCOL
Allen Bradley (Rockwell)	DeviceNet, ControNet, DF1, Data Highway +, Data Highway 485
Siemens	Profibus
Modicon	MODBUS, MODBUS Plus, MODBUS TCP/IP

Many of these protocols are proprietary. In the 1990s, control industry groups and standards organizations began to develop open protocols for control systems that would be nonproprietary and not exclusive to one manufacturer. Then, as the Internet gained popularity, companies sought to take advantage of the protocols and tools developed for the Internet, such as the TCP/IP family of protocols and Internet browsers. In addition, manufacturers and open standards organizations modified the highly popular and efficient Ethernet LAN technology for use in implementing data acquisition and control local area networks.

Background Technologies of the SCADA Protocols

In order for any entities to communicate, a protocol for that communication has to be established. A protocol defines the format of the messages and the rules for the exchange of the messages.

High-level models are used to define where the protocols are applied and to compartmentalize the functions required to send and receive messages. The layered architecture model has been widely adopted and is very effective. In this model, the elements necessary for communication are divided into layers with defined interfaces between each layer. Two of the most widely used layered communication reference models are the open systems interconnection (OSI) model and the transmission control protocol/Internet protocol (TCP/IP) model.

Overview of the OSI Model

The open systems interconnection (OSI) reference model was developed by the International Standards Organization (ISO) in the beginning of the 1980s. In this model, the data from a higher-level layer is encapsulated by the next lower layer as it is passed from higher- to lower-level layers. For example, a packet of data from a higher level will be encapsulated by the next lower layer by adding header information around the data packet. Figure 3-1 illustrates a basic encapsulation process.

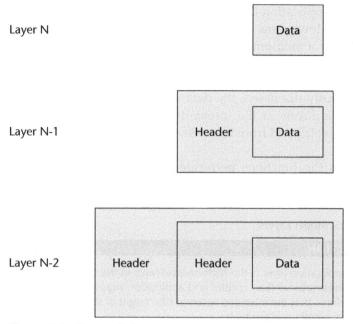

Figure 3-1 Encapsulation

The OSI model layers are depicted in Figure 3-2.

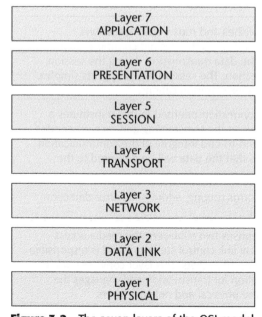

Figure 3-2 The seven layers of the OSI model

In the OSI model, the application layer, layer 7, is the interface to the user. Data traverses the model downward from layer 7 to layer 1, where a message packet is transmitted over a medium such as a wire or optical fiber cable as electrical or optical pulses, respectively. On the receiving end, the reverse procedure takes place, with the message packet traversing the model from layer 1 up to layer 7. As previously discussed, the data is encapsulated as it travels down through the model layers at the transmitting node. At the receiving node, the encapsulation is stripped from the message as it works its way up to layer 7.

Table 3-2 summarizes the functions performed in each layer of the OSI model.

Table 3-2 Functions of OSI Model Layers

LAYER	FUNCTION
7-Application	The application layer is the highest-level layer in the OSI model. It performs network flow control and application support functions. It confirms that the intended receiver (the target of the communication) is available.
6-Presentation	The presentation layer performs conversions and translations for the application layer. It also performs encryption, decryption, and compression operations. For example, this layer translates data coded in the American Standard Code for Information Exchange (ASCII) and the Extended Binary Coded Decimal Interchange Code (EBCDIC).
5-Session	The session layer establishes and runs network sessions. Specifically, this layer establishes the desired communication connection, manages the data transmission during the session, and releases the connection. The session layer supports simplex, half duplex, and full duplex communications.
4-Transport	The transport layer is connection-oriented in that it institutes a logical connection between the transmitting and receiving nodes. This layer establishes end-to-end integrity of the communication session and guarantees that the data will be delivered to the receiving host.
3-Network	The network layer performs routing, addressing, error detection, and node traffic control.
2-Data Link	The data link layer comprises two sublayers, the media access control (MAC) and logical link control sublayers, and is responsible for error-free transmission of packets. This layer converts packets into bit form in preparation for transmission and manages the data frames between the physical and network layers.

Table 3-2 *(continued)*

LAYER	FUNCTION
1-Physical	The physical layer connects the computer to the physical network transmission media. As such, it is responsible for converting the packet data to electrical signals or optical pulses and also defines the electrical and mechanical interfaces to the network. EIA-232 and EIA-422 specifications are examples of such standard interfaces.

Each layer in the OSI model uses specific protocols to implement its functions. Table 3-3 provides examples of some of the protocols associated with each layer.

Table 3-3 OSI Protocols

LAYER	PROTOCOLS
7-Application	FTP (file transfer protocol): Supports transfer of files between computers. SMTP (simple mail transport protocol): Supports the sending and receiving of e-mail messages. SNMP (simple network management protocol): Collects network information and presents it to network management consoles.
6-Presentation	HTTP (hypertext transfer protocol): The protocol used by the World Wide Web (WWW). HTTP is a stateless protocol in that it executes its commands without any knowledge of its prior state and any previously executed commands. HTTP defines the formats for message transmission and how browsers react to instructions. JPEG (Joint Photographic Experts Group): A defined standard for graphics. MPEG (Motion Pictures Experts Group): Standard for coding and compression of motion picture video.
5-Session	RPC (remote procedure call): In the client-server model, a protocol that supports a request for service from one computer on a network from another computer on the network. NFS (network file system): Supports file sharing
4-Transport	TCP (Transmission Control Protocol): Provides stream-oriented, reliable connections, error correction, and flow control, which prevent buffer overflows. UDP (user datagram protocol): Unlike TCP, UDP does not perform error correction; UDP delivers messages on a best-effort basis.

(continued)

Table 3-3   *(continued)*

LAYER	PROTOCOLS
3-Network	IP (Internet protocol): Assigns IP addresses of the sender and recipient to data packets to be used in routing the message to its intended receiver. IP does not guarantee reliable delivery of data packets. ICMP (Internet control message protocol): A management protocol used to determine transmission routes from a source to a destination host and to check the availability of a host to receive messages. One of the ICMP utilities is PING, which is used to check the connection of hosts to the network.
2-Data Link	ARP (address resolution protocol): Determines the MAC hardware address of a destination host from its IP address. PPP (point-to-point protocol): A full-duplex, encapsulation protocol for sending IP messages over point-to-point links.
1-Physical	EIA-422-B (RS-422): Electronic Industries Association standard that defines the electrical characteristics of a balanced interface circuit that is designed for high common-mode noise rejection and data rates less than 0.5 Mbps. EIA -232C (RS-232C): Electronic Industries Association standard for serial binary data exchange.

Overview of the TCP/IP Model

The transmission control protocol/Internet protocol (TCP/IP) was developed in the 1970s by the U.S. Department of Defense to implement reliable network communications. TCP/IP powers the Internet and the Internet's various capabilities are based on TCP/IP protocols.

The OSI model was developed after TCP/IP, but it attempted to maintain some similarities to the TCP/IP model. The four TCP/IP layers are illustrated in Figure 3-3 and their functions are given in Table 3-4.

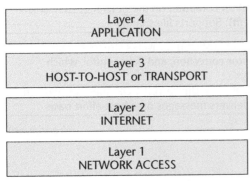

Figure 3-3   The TCP/IP layered architecture

Table 3-4 Functions of TCP/IP Model Layers

LAYER	FUNCTION
4-Application	As in the OSI model layer 7, the application layer is the interface to the user. It supports the user network applications and performs flow control and error recovery.
3-Host-to-Host or Transport	The host-to-host layer assembles data in packets, provides for connection-oriented end-to-end communication, supports error-free and reliable delivery of message packets, and controls the network data flow.
2-Internet	The Internet layer performs routing and addressing.
1-Network Access	The network access layer includes the functions of the data link and physical layers of the OSI model. It converts packets into bits for transmission over the physical medium and is responsible for error-free delivery of frames.

The TCP/IP layers also incorporate protocols to perform the layers' functions. Examples of these protocols are listed in Table 3-5.

Table 3-5 TCP/IP Protocols

LAYER	PROTOCOLS
4-Application	FTP (file transfer protocol): Supports transfer of files between computers. SMTP (simple mail transport protocol): Supports the sending and receiving of e-mail messages. SNMP (simple network management protocol): Collects network information and presents it to network management consoles. Telnet: Using terminal emulation, Telnet provides a client with the capability to access a remote computer.
3-Host-to-Host or Transport	TCP (transmission control protocol): Provides stream-oriented, reliable connections, error correction, and flow control, which prevent buffer overflows. UDP (user datagram protocol): Unlike TCP, UDP does not perform error correction and delivers messages on a best effort basis.
2-Internet	IP (Internet protocol): Assigns IP addresses of the sender and recipient to data packets to be used in routing the message to its intended receiver. IP does not guarantee reliable delivery of data packets. ICMP (Internet control message protocol): A management protocol used to determine transmission routes from a source to a destination host and to check the availability of a host to receive messages. One of the ICMP utilities is PING, which is used to check the connection of hosts to the network.

(continued)

Table 3-5   *(continued)*

LAYER	PROTOCOLS
2-Internet	ARP (address resolution protocol): Determines the MAC hardware address of a destination host from its IP address. PPP (point-to-point protocol): A full-duplex, encapsulation protocol for sending IP messages over point-to-point links.
1-Network Access	IEEE 802.2 Logical Link Control: Manages data link communications between devices and performs error checking on frames received. EIA-422-B (RS-422): Electronic Industries Association standard that defines the electrical characteristics of a balanced interface circuit that is designed to for high common-mode noise rejection and data rates less than 0.5 Mbps. EIA -232C (RS-232C): Electronic Industries Association standard for serial binary data exchange.

Using this background on the layered models and associated protocols, we can now explore the related SCADA models and protocols in the following sections.

SCADA Protocols

The SCADA system protocols evolved from propriety hardware and software designed specifically for SCADA systems. The protocols were developed out of necessity to serve the burgeoning market for computer applications in real-time control situations. Then, in an effort to take advantage of new networking developments, SCADA protocols incorporated versions of Internet and local area network technologies. This move led to some standardization, but also exposed SCADA systems to attacks commonly used against these technologies in IT environments.

The MODBUS Model

In the late 1970s, Modicon, Incorporated, developed the MODBUS protocol. MODBUS is positioned in layer 7 (the application layer of the OSI model) and supports client-server communications among Modicon PLCs and other networked devices. The MODBUS protocol defines the methods for a PLC to obtain access to another PLC, for a PLC to respond to other devices, and means for detecting and reporting errors. The protocol supports other protocols such as asynchronous master-slave transmission, Modicon MODBUS Plus, and Ethernet. In order to take advantage of the supporting tools, hardware, and software that are used for the Internet, MODBUS/TCP was also developed. It too is based on the OSI model, although not all layers are used. The communications layers of the various MODBUS protocol implementations are given in Figure 3-4.

A typical MODBUS transaction comprises the following steps:

1. The MODBUS Application protocol sets the format of a client-initiated request.

2. A function code in a MODBUS *data unit*, as the message packet is called, directs the server to execute a specific action.

3. A data field in the message provides additional information used by the server to perform the requested action.

4. If there are no errors in the exchange, the server completes the requested action, typically sending data back to the client.

5. If an error occurs, the server reads an exception code in the data unit to determine the next action to be performed.

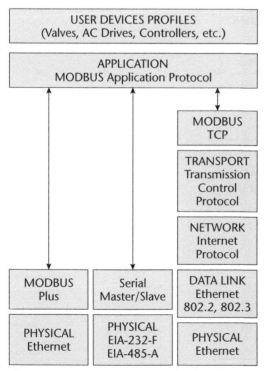

Figure 3-4 MODBUS communications layers

The DNP3 Protocol

DNP3 is an open SCADA protocol that is used for serial or IP communication between control devices. It is widely used by utilities such as water companies and electricity suppliers for the exchange of data and control instructions between *master* control stations and remote computers or controllers called *out-stations*. Typical commands issued by the master control station are "open a valve," "start a motor," and "provide data on a particular control station." The master control station might also provide analog output signals to the outstation.

An outstation provides the master control station with information such as pressures, status of a circuit breaker or recloser, analog signals representing such items as temperature or power, and information files.

DNP3 has also adapted to Internet technologies by using TCP/IP for exchange of DNP3 messages. A typical DNP3 TCP/IP layered architecture showing the exchange of data between a master control station and outstation is given in Figure 3-5.

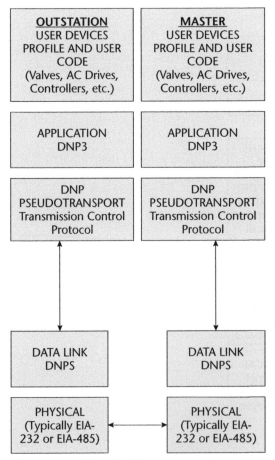

Figure 3-5   DNP3 TCP/IP data exchange

A DNP3 frame comprises a header and data. The header comprises the following:

- DNP3 source device address
- DNP3 destination device address
- Frame size
- Data link control information

The data portion of the header contains the data that traverses the layers from the highest to the lowest layer.

UCA 2.0 and IEC61850 Standards

In the early 1990s, the Electric Power Research Institute (EPRI) decided that an effort was needed to define a more robust standard than DNP3 to serve the SCADA needs of the electric utilities. The result was the Utility Communications Architecture (UCA). UCA version 2.0 is a family of communications protocols aimed at meeting the needs of electric utilities. UCA 2.0 is based on the Manufacturing Message Specification (MMS) from ISO Standards ISO 9506-1:2000 and ISO 9506-2:2000. In 1999, UCA 2.0 migrated to IEC Standard IEC61850 for substation automation. IEC61850 is part of a Common Information Model (CIM) developed by IEC Technical Committee 57 that also includes the following standards:

- IEC61970: Power systems and programming interfaces for integrating utility applications
- IEC61968: Distribution equipment and processes
- IEC60870-5: Distribution
- IEC60870-6: Transmission

IEC61850 is a layered architecture standard that separates the functionality required for electric utility applications from the lower-level networking tasks. The layered architecture illustrating the separation of functions is shown in Figure 3-6.

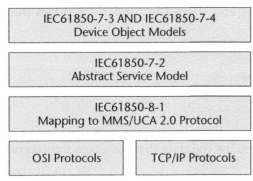

Figure 3-6   IEC61850 layered architecture

Controller Area Network

Controller area network (CAN) protocols (ISO Standard 11898-1) were developed for the automotive industry by Robert Bosch, GMBH, in the mid 1980s for use in serial communications up to 1 Mbps. CAN supports up to 110 nodes on a two-wire, half-duplex network.

The protocols operate at layer 1, the physical layer, and layer 2, the data link layer, of the OSI model.

CAN communications are based on the Ethernet carrier sense multiple access with collision detection (CSMA/CD) method. With CSMA/CD, multiple devices compete to transmit information over a common bus. When a device senses that the bus is free (no carrier signal on the bus), it tries to transmit over the bus. In the event another device tries to communicate over the bus at the same time, the devices detect this collision, back-off, and try again at a random time later. Thus, with this approach, specific transmission times across the network cannot be guaranteed. To compensate for this situation, CAN provides transmission priorities to nodes using the CSMA/CD + AMP (arbitration on message priority) scheme. CSMA/CD + AMP employs a unique identifier that includes a priority rating in a message instead of the source and destination node addresses as used in the conventional CSMA/CD arbitration method. The lower the value of the identifier, the higher the priority that is assigned to the message. The length of this identifier varies, being 11 bits in CAN specification part A and 29 bits long for CAN specification part B. Using the identifier priority value, the CAN transmission algorithm involves the following steps:

1. A message with the highest priority identifier is granted access to transmit.

2. Each node traversed by a message examines the unique identifier to determine whether the message is being sent to that node.

3. If a message is intended for that node, the node processes the message. Messages with a lower-priority identifier are transmitted after higher-priority messages according to their identifier values.

Control and Information Protocol

The Common Industrial Protocol (CIP) is an open family of protocols that is implemented in the application, presentation, and session layers of the OSI model. Thus, CIP forms a common upper layer of protocols that can be used above different lower layers, such as those employing EtherNet/IP, DeviceNet, and ControlNet, all of which are discussed in following sections. It also includes a messaging protocol that supports explicit messaging and I/O. CIP is maintained by ControlNet International (CI) and the Open DeviceNet Vendor Association (ODVA).

The value of CIP is that it makes predefined objects and communication standards available to the lower layers of the OSI model. CIP comprises communication objects, which are used to define maximum data values, type and characteristics of the connection, and timing of the connection. It also supplies a 46-class object library, which includes control supervisor objects, port objects, identity objects, analog output point objects, parameter objects, discrete input objects, position sensor objects, and AC/DC drive objects.

The relationships among CIP, CAN, and other protocols are illustrated in Figure 3-7.

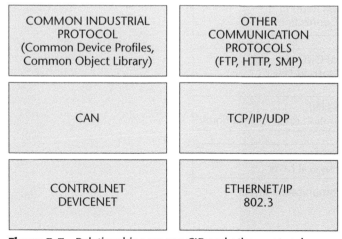

Figure 3-7 Relationships among CIP and other protocols

DeviceNet

DeviceNet is an open standard that is used to connect equipment such as motor starters, sensors, valve controls, displays, operator interfaces, and higher level control computers and PLCs. DeviceNet is based on the CAN protocols. It also uses the CIP family of protocols, including its object libraries and object profiles for configuration and control of the equipment and to obtain data from the local devices through the CAN protocols at the data link and physical layers. In order to accomplish an information exchange, for example, DeviceNet establishes a connection instance using an identity object, a message router object, a DeviceNet object, and a connection object. The identity object contains information such as the device profile, revision number, and vendor information. The message router object routes messages to the proper destination and the DeviceNet object stores lower-layer DeviceNet information such as the MAC identification number. The connection object manages the messaging connection. DeviceNet supports communication rates of 125kbps, 250kbps, and 500kbps for up to 64 nodes.

Figure 3-8 illustrates the DeviceNet layers and their use with CIP.

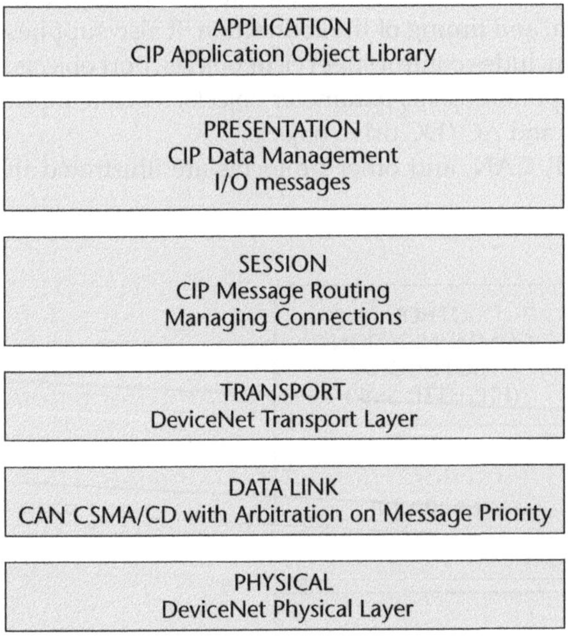

```
┌─────────────────────────────────────────────────┐
│              APPLICATION                         │
│         CIP Application Object Library           │
└─────────────────────────────────────────────────┘

┌─────────────────────────────────────────────────┐
│              PRESENTATION                        │
│           CIP Data Management                    │
│              I/O messages                        │
└─────────────────────────────────────────────────┘

┌─────────────────────────────────────────────────┐
│                SESSION                           │
│           CIP Message Routing                    │
│           Managing Connections                   │
└─────────────────────────────────────────────────┘

┌─────────────────────────────────────────────────┐
│               TRANSPORT                          │
│          DeviceNet Transport Layer               │
└─────────────────────────────────────────────────┘

┌─────────────────────────────────────────────────┐
│               DATA LINK                          │
│   CAN CSMA/CD with Arbitration on Message Priority│
└─────────────────────────────────────────────────┘

┌─────────────────────────────────────────────────┐
│                PHYSICAL                          │
│          DeviceNet Physical Layer                │
└─────────────────────────────────────────────────┘
```

Figure 3-8   DeviceNet communication layers

ControlNet

ControlNet is an open network for use in real-time, deterministic SCADA applications. It also uses the CIP protocol object capabilities and can support up to 99 nodes on the network at a data rate of 5 Mbps. It is designed for applications that comprise multiple controllers and operator interfaces, and it supports the exchange of real-time I/O data as well as messaging information.

The determinism of ControlNet comes from the incorporation of the Concurrent Time Domain Multiple Access (CTDMA) algorithm that allows a node on the network to transmit at a specified interval called the *network update time* or NUT. Thus, critical information is transmitted during a NUT interval while noncritical information is sent in unscheduled periods, as they are available. CTDMA is illustrated in Figure 3-9.

The ControlNet communication layers are given in Figure 3-10.

EtherNet/IP

EtherNet/IP also applies CIP by encoding CIP messages in Ethernet frames. In addition to the basic CIP object classes, EtherNet/IP uses a TCP/IP object for implementing the TCP/IP protocol and an Ethernet link object comprising parameters for establishing an EtherNet/IP link. CIP operates at the application layer providing the application object library, at the presentation layer providing messaging services, and at the session layer supporting message routing and connection management. The session layer interfaces to the transport and network layers, which perform encapsulation and apply either the TCP or the UDP protocol at the transport layer and the IP protocol at the network layer. The data completes the downward transition at the data link layer, which implements CSMA/CD and the Ethernet physical layer, which connects to the transmission medium.

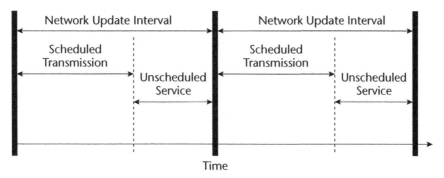

Figure 3-9   ControlNet CTDMA timing diagram

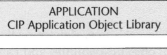

| APPLICATION |
| CIP Application Object Library |

| PRESENTATION |
| CIP Data Management |
| I/O messages |

| SESSION |
| CIP Message Routing |
| Managing Connections |

| TRANSPORT |
| ControlNet Transport Layer |

| DATA LINK |
| CTDMA |

| PHYSICAL |
| ControlNet Physical Layer |

Figure 3-10   ControlNet

Because the Ethernet uses CSMA/CD, which operates by detecting colli-sions, backing off, and trying to resend at random intervals, communications are not deterministic. This situation poses problems for real-time data acquisi-tion and control. In order to mitigate this situation, EtherNet/IP applies layer 2 switches to partition collision domains into single nodes or small groups. This division significantly reduces CSMA/CD collisions. Also, advances in Ethernet technology, especially Fast Ethernet (100 Mbps) and Gigabit Ethernet (10 Gbps), drastically reduce the nondeterministic communication latency times.

A third mitigating factor is the availability of the user datagram protocol (UDP), which transmits packets on a best-effort basis and does not carry the overhead associated with TCP transmission, which confirms the communica-tion connection and checks for errors in transmission.

Finally, the IEEE has developed the 802.1P specification for prioritizing net-work traffic by incorporating a 3-bit header field that prioritizes messages and allows for the grouping of packets into different priority traffic classes. Figure 3-11 shows the EtherNet/IP layers and their relationship to CIP.

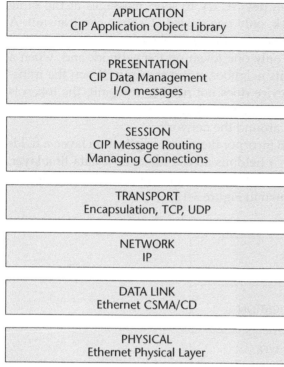

Figure 3-11   EtherNet/IP

FFB

The flexible function block (FFB) process is a control half-duplex bus network. It was developed by the Fieldbus Foundation, which is a consortium of 130 automation organizations. The goal of the consortium was to develop an open, two-wire international standard for process automation applications. It is particularly useful for controlling devices such as valves and transmitter devices.

In operation, each device on an FFB network taps into the two-wire bus structure. Logically, FFB operates as a 31.25 Kbps master-slave network, but functions for a brief period as a token-passing scheme. In the master-slave communication model, a master or primary device controls a number of slaves or secondary devices. The master sends control signals to the slave devices and they respond according to the control instructions received. The slaves can send information back to the master for storage, interpretation, and processing. The token passing scheme is a method used to arbitrate among devices that desire to communicate on a network. Unlike the CSMA/CD approach where collisions can occur when devices try to send messages at the same time, in a token passing network, only one device at a time can transmit. A device can transmit when it receives an electronic token (similar to a message) that is passed around. There is only one token on the network and, when a device receives the token from its neighbor, it can transmit. When the transmission is complete or if the device does not need to transmit, the token is passed on to the next device. Then, the next device can transmit. This process continues as the token is passed around the network.

Relative to the OSI model, FFB incorporates a user application layer, a fieldbus message specification layer, a fieldbus access sublayer, a data link layer, and a physical layer. Layers 3 through 6 of the corresponding OSI model are not used. The FFB layers are shown in Figure 3-12.

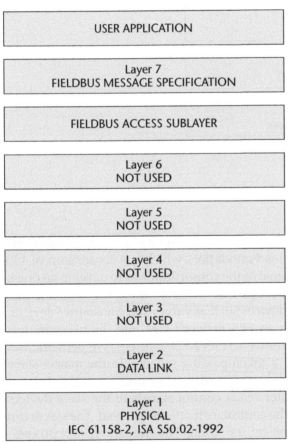

Figure 3-12 Foundation fieldbus layered architecture

In the FFB layers, the application layer comprises the Fieldbus Message Specification (FMS) and the Fieldbus Access Sublayer (FAS). FMS provides for the exchange of messages among applications and FAS supports the FMS. The data link layer uses a link active scheduler (LAS) to control the sending of fieldbus messages. The LAS is the mechanism that FFB uses to provide determinism by maintaining a list of network transmission times for all devices on the network. Devices transmit at their designated transmit times and, if there is time available between these scheduled transmit times, devices can transmit during these unscheduled times. The FFB physical layer follows IEC Standard 61158-2 and ISA Standard S50.02-1992. The electrical characteristics of this layer include the use of Manchester biphase encoding of the digital signals and a ± 10-mA current loop. Manchester encoding uses pulse transitions to represent binary ones and zeros instead of pulse voltage or current levels. The FFB physical layer also provides power supply voltages from 9 to 32 volts.

Profibus

Profibus (Process Fieldbus) is an open fieldbus serial network standard for use in time-critical control and data acquisition applications. It falls under the European international fieldbus standard, EN 50 170, and defines the functional, electrical, and mechanical characteristics of a serial fieldbus. Profibus is similar to the Foundation fieldbus, but provides transmission rates of 31.25 Kbps, 1Mbps, and 2.5 Mbps in the physical layer.

Because Profibus is an open standard, it can accommodate devices from different manufacturers. Profibus resides at the application, data link, and physical layers of the OSI model. It provides determinism for real-time control applications and supports multimaster and master-slave communication networks.

There are three versions of Profibus, which are summarized in the following list:

- **Profibus Process Automation (PA):** Connects data acquisition and control devices on a common serial bus and supports reliable, intrinsically safe implementations. It also provides power to field devices through the bus. Profibus PA uses the basic functions and extensions available in Profibus DP.

- **Profibus Factory Automation (Decentralized Peripherals — DP):** Provides high-speed communication between control systems and decentralized control devices. It uses different physical layer standards than those employed by Profibus PA. Optional and upward compatible extensions have been added to Profibus DP. The extended version is denoted as Profibus-DPV1 and includes diagnostics, alarm messaging, and parameterization.

■ **Profibus Fieldbus Message Specification (FMS):** Developed to support a large number of applications and higher-level network interconnections among applications at average transmission rates. It offers a large selection of functions and is, generally, more complicated to implement than Profibus PA or Profibus DP. The three Profibus versions with their primary characteristics are given in Figure 3-13.

Figure 3-14 illustrates the communication architectures of the Profibus versions and shows their relationship in the OSI seven-layer model.

Figure 3-13   Profibus versions

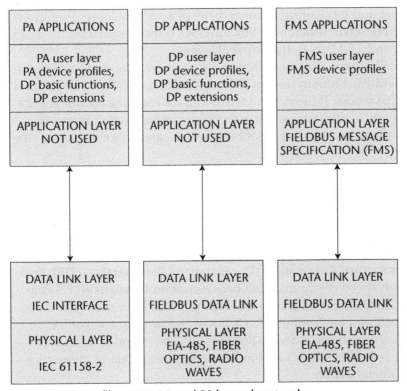

Figure 3-14   Profibus FMS, DP, and PA layered protocols

In Figure 3-14, the physical layers use either the EIA-485 standard or the IEC 61158-2 standard. If desired, all three Profibus versions can use the same bus line if they employ EIA-485 in the physical layer. However, if the application requires intrinsically safe circuitry, IEC 61158-2 must be used. EIA-485 provides transmission rates of 9.6 to 1200 Kbps while IEC 61158-2 operates at 31.25 Kbps.

The Security Implications of the SCADA Protocols

Most networks, including SCADA networks, have some common security issues and corresponding controls. An important consideration for SCADA networks is that they cannot afford nondeterministic delays, security mechanisms that require large memory capacities, locking out of operators, and relatively long processing times. However, some of the fundamental security measures available to SCADA systems are similar to those used for OSI and TCP/IP layered architectures. Network best practices include protecting the confidentiality, integrity, availability (CIA) of data along with providing nonrepudiation, authentication, and access services.

Firewalls

A key security element of protection that is required of any network connected to an untrusted network, such as the Internet, is a firewall. A firewall provides protection against viruses, worms, and other types of malicious code as well as from network intrusions. An issue with firewalls applied to SCADA systems is that most firewalls do not support handling of SCADA protocols. This situation is being researched by a number of organizations and some SCADA-aware firewalls are under development.

A typical network configuration employing a firewall between an internal LAN and the Internet is given in Figure 3-15.

The three common types of firewalls are packet-filtering firewalls, stateful inspection firewalls, and proxy firewalls.

Packet-Filtering Firewalls

A packet-filtering firewall operates at layer 3, the network layer, of the OSI model and uses filtering criteria to decide whether to permit or deny packets entry into the local network. The parts of the packet that are examined are the source IP address, the destination IP address, and the Internet protocols carried by the packet.

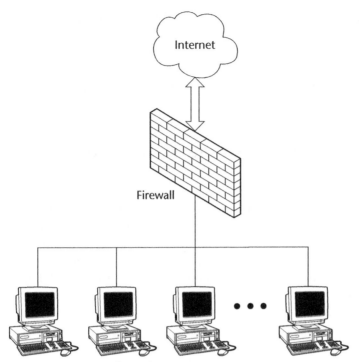

Figure 3-15   Firewall employment

By checking the source IP address of the incoming packet, a packet-filtering firewall can block packets from unwanted IP sources, such as untrusted hosts, advertisers, and spam mailers. The filtering is based on database files known as access control lists (ACLs) that are stored by the firewall.

By using similar sets of rules, a packet-filtering firewall can prohibit traffic from being sent to an internal IP destination address. This action can prevent messages from being sent to computers containing highly classified information and reduce the number of messages sent to specific hosts.

A third filter is based on examining the Internet protocol carried by the packet. Some of the protocols that are examined are normal Internet protocol (IP), address resolution protocol (ARP), reverse address resolution protocol (RARP), transmission control protocol (TCP), user datagram protocol (UDP), and the Internet control message protocol (ICMP). The firewall can block packets with specific protocols from entering the trusted network.

Stateful Inspection Firewalls

A stateful inspection firewall stores and maintains information from an incoming packet in a dynamic memory state table. These tables store the source and destination connection information associated with the packet and use rules to determine if the communication should be allowed to proceed. Connection information includes the destination address and port, and the source address and port. Because the speed of operation of a stateful inspection firewall is determined by the time it takes to perform a more detailed examination of the packet state and the number of connections handled, queuing delays might occur that would be detrimental to the operation of a SCADA system.

Proxy Firewalls

Proxy or application layer firewalls operate at layer 7 of the OSI model. In the dictionary, a proxy is defined as a person authorized to act for another; an agent or substitute. Thus, proxy software can be placed between a user and a server to conceal the identity of the user. The server sees the proxy and cannot identify the user. The scenario is also true in the reverse situation where the user interacts with the proxy software in front of the server and cannot identify the server or its associated network. A proxy firewall is effective in shielding a network from an untrusted outside network, such as the Internet.

Demilitarized Zone

Firewalls can be used to implement security network architectures that are effective for SCADA systems. These architectures are based on the concept of a demilitarized zone or DMZ. A DMZ is a region that provides a separation between an external or public network and an internal or private network. In order for a firewall to support a DMZ, it must have multiple external interfaces and corresponding access control lists, where necessary. Several different architectures use DMZs, but there are two that are particularly applicable to data acquisition and control environments. These architectures are a single firewall DMZ and a dual firewall DMZ. They can serve the purpose of separating a corporate enterprise network from the control network while providing a connection for both to a public network such as the Internet.

Single Firewall DMZ

In a single firewall DMZ, a firewall is used to filter data packets from, for example, an enterprise network to the local control network and from an external network. The DMZ contains the elements that have to be accessed by the enterprise computers as well as the connection to the outside, public network. This architecture is shown in Figure 3-16.

Because there is no firewall between the DMZ and control network, the control network is potentially vulnerable if the DMZ is penetrated by an attack from the external network or the through the enterprise network.

Dual Firewall DMZ

The security of a SCADA network can be increased by adding a second firewall between the control network and the DMZ. This arrangement implements a dual firewall DMZ. See Figure 3-17.

General Firewall Rules for Different Services

Because of the stringent requirements of SCADA systems with regard to timing, availability, and data processing, firewall rules have to be tailored for the various protocols and network services. The Industrial Automation Open Networking Association (IAONA) developed protocol guidelines (*The IAONA Handbook for Network Security-Draft/RFC v0.4*, Magdeburg, Germany, 2003) for network services that accommodate the unique SCADA system characteristics. These guidelines for communications with SCADA systems are summarized in Table 3-6. The services provided by the protocols are summarized in Tables 3-3 and 3-5.

ENTERPRISE NETWORK

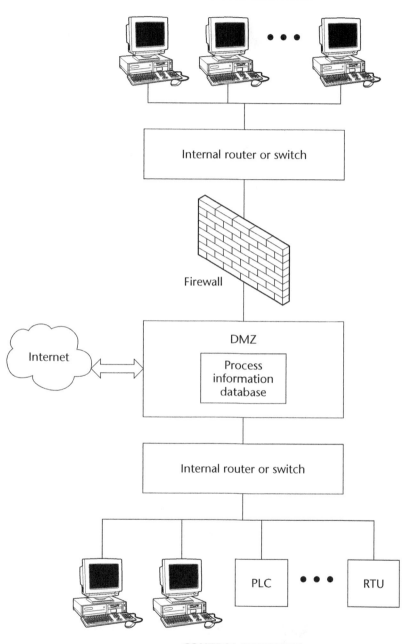

CONTROL NETWORK

Figure 3-16 Single firewall DMZ for SCADA

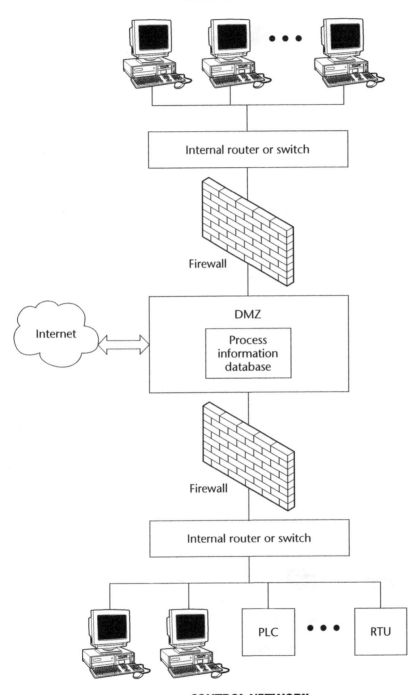

Figure 3-17 Dual firewall DMZ for SCADA

Table 3-6 Firewall Protocol Rules for Different Services to SCADA Systems

PROTOCOL	RULE
File Transfer Protocol (FTP)	FTP permitted on outbound communications only. Should employ an encrypted VPN tunnel and token-based two-factor authentication. Inbound communications not permitted.
Trivial File Transfer Protocol (TFTP)	TFTP should not be permitted.
Simple Mail Transfer Protocol (SMTP)	Outbound e-mail messages permitted; inbound e-mail messages blocked.
Telnet	Outbound communications should employ an encrypted VPN tunnel to known devices. Inbound communications should employ an encrypted VPN tunnel and token-based two-factor authentication.
HyperText Transfer Protocol (HTTP)	Inbound communications should not be permitted unless necessary. If required, HTTP should be used with the secure sockets layer (SSL) protocol (HTTP/S). SSL provides encryption and authentication capabilities. Communications from the enterprise should be configured in the firewall to block Java and other scripts.
Simple Network Management Protocol (SNMP)	SNMP communications should not be permitted unless implemented over a different, secure network.
SCADA and Industrial Protocols	Because security was not considered in the design of these protocols, communications should be prohibited to and from the enterprise network and limited to the process control networks and related process control information networks.

Virtual Private Networks

A virtual private network or VPN is a highly effective solution for transmitting data securely over the Internet or a wide area network. A VPN is said to create a secure *tunnel* in an untrusted network and through a firewall, through which sensitive data can be transmitted.

The tunnel is created by encapsulating, or by encapsulating and encrypting, the data and then transmitting it over the network. Typically, data is encapsulated by adding a header and then encrypted before being transmitted. A VPN securely connecting two networks is illustrated in Figure 3-18.

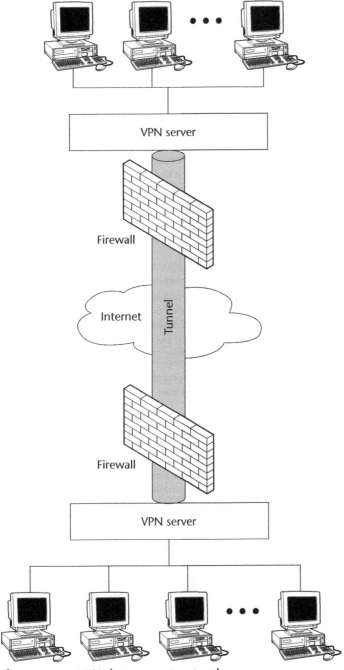

Figure 3-18   A VPN between two networks

Summary

Protocols supporting real-time data acquisition and control in manufacturing and process control applications began as proprietary solutions offered by control equipment manufacturers. These protocols and associated communication buses met the needs of users and were widely applied. The next steps in the evolution of SCADA protocols were the development of open-standard protocols and the adoption of Ethernet and Internet technologies. With these changes, particularly the use of the Internet architectural elements and connections to transmit and receive data involving SCADA systems, security issues are now of concern. Proper use of the SCADA protocols coupled with network security devices such as firewalls can provide SCADA users with secure, efficient, and cost-effective communication means.

Summary

SCADA Vulnerabilities and Attacks

With the advent of the terrorist threat to many nations' critical infrastructures, SCADA systems are no longer low-visibility, anonymous entities working silently to control industrial and commercial operations. Even though many organizations employing SCADA systems are reluctant to admit it, data acquisition and control networks are becoming attractive targets for malicious individuals, belligerent nations, terrorist groups, curious hackers, and, perhaps, an organization's competitors. Add the potential for natural disasters and today's SCADA systems are more vulnerable than ever before to disruption and compromise. This chapter explores the vulnerabilities and risks associated with SCADA systems, the changing mentality of SCADA network users, attack paths to SCADA components, and the potential actions that can be taken against plants employing SCADA technology. The chapter concludes with a discussion of a new application of honeypots and honeynets to protect SCADA systems and capture relevant information on attackers' approaches and methods that can be used to develop SCADA security controls that are more effective.

The Myth of SCADA Invulnerability

As discussed in Chapters 1 and 3, SCADA systems evolved from proprietary hardware and software platforms used in the 1960s to acquire data from and control real-time operations. The networks and protocols used in SCADA systems were also proprietary and customized to meet the specific needs of the industrial world. Over the next 20 years, typical SCADA architectures included a computer such as the Digital Equipment Corporation (DEC) PDP 11 running a real-time operating system such as RSX/11M, a DEC VAX running VMS, and proprietary PLCs programmed with ladder logic.

Because there was no Internet or World Wide Web at the time, and the SCADA systems were self-contained, they were generally safe against malicious intrusions and attacks from the outside. However, the SCADA system components were still vulnerable to threats from the inside. Even when the Internet emerged and SCADA systems began to incorporate standard hardware and software platforms that had known vulnerabilities, the mentality of most SCADA users remained the same. The SCADA community believed that external hackers were not interested in their applications and probably did not know much about the existence of SCADA systems. This thinking was reinforced by the fact that through the 1980s and early 1990s, the most SCADA security incidents were initiated by disgruntled employees or were the result of accidents. At that time, SCADA systems were not considered IT systems, and therefore, were assumed relatively less vulnerable to IT-type cyberattacks. Even to this day, many SCADA systems are perceived as either invulnerable to cyberattacks or uninteresting to potential hackers. For example, Scott Berinato, in his article entitled "Debunking the Threat to Water Utilities" in the March 15, 2002, issue of *CIO* magazine, describes the near impossibility of hackers penetrating the Massachusetts Water Resource Authority (MWRA) facilities and operations center in Chelsea, Massachusetts. Berinato describes the MWRA's sophisticated safeguards against cyberattacks and states, "most public utilities rely on a highly customized SCADA system. No two are the same, so hacking them requires specific knowledge. In this case, knowledge of the MWRA's design and access to that customized software." While it is true that the MWRA has deployed extensive security measures, it is imprudent to assume that the risks of malicious attacks are nonexistent.

In a related sidebar article, "The Truth About Cyber Terrorism," in the same issue of *CIO* magazine, Berinato further states that "CIOs and security experts are beginning to challenge the assumption that a hack on the nation's critical infrastructure will be the next big terrorist outrage. In fact, cyber terrorism may not be nearly as worrisome as some would make it. That's because it is utterly defensible."

Many others in the scientific, engineering, and information security communities hold a contrary view. In an October 2003 keynote address to the National Science Foundation (NSF) Workshop on Critical Infrastructure Protection for SCADA & IT, Dr. Arden Bement, director of the National Institute of

Standards & Technology, listed the following incidents demonstrating the vulnerability of critical infrastructure SCADA systems:

- An out-of-control cascade of events left eight states and part of Canada and some 50 million people without electric power in August 2003.

- In the spring of 2001, hackers broke into computer systems of CAL-ISO, California's primary electric power grid operator, and apparently were not discovered for 17 days.

- A wireless link to the SCADA system for the Queensland, Australia, Maroochy Shire sewage control system in 2000 was exploited by one Vitek Boden. This attack caused millions of gallons of sewage to be dumped into Maroochy waterways over a four-month period.

- When security consultant Paul Blomgren and his associates were hired to assess SCADA vulnerabilities at a large southwestern power utility with about four million customers, they were able to penetrate the power station's operational control network and computer systems through wireless connections from laptops in a vehicle parked outside of the plant.

In the same address, Dr. Bement noted, "The notion that SCADA systems are highly customized, highly technical, and therefore the guys in the black hats won't be able to figure them out is something Eric Byres of the British Columbia Institute of Technology (BCIT) calls the 'Myth of Obscurity.' Forget it. SCADA documents have been recovered from al Qaeda safe houses in Afghanistan. . . . There is no security through obscurity."

Other SCADA system attacks further illustrate the diversity of targets and penetration techniques:

- A 1994 attack on a Tempe, Arizona, water and electricity provider (the Salt River Project)

- A 2001 distributed -denial -of-service (DDoS) attack against the Port of Houston Web-based systems by attackers through the computer of Aaron Caffrey, who successfully defended himself as an unknowing victim whose computer was used as a bounce site

- On the Ohio Davis-Besse nuclear power plant process computer, a 2003 Slammer worm attack, which disabled a nuclear safety monitoring system for over five hours

- An attack in 2003 by the Sobig virus on CSX dispatching and signaling systems that disrupted freight and commuter rail service among Washington, D.C., Virginia, and Maryland

SCADA Risk Components

The control components of SCADA systems are optimized to provide deterministic, real-time performance at a reasonable cost. Thus, there are little excess memory and computing cycles available for executing other functions not considered necessary for the basic SCADA mission. As a result, SCADA system manufacturers view additional computing tasks, including information system security, as burdens on the computing capacity that could interfere with the proper operation of the system. Information system security was not inherent in SCADA protocols because, when the protocols were developed, SCADA systems were usually operating in closed environments with no vulnerable connections to the outside world. In today's SCADA applications, the opposite is true. SCADA systems are connected to corporate IT networks and use protocols and computing platforms that are under attack in the conventional IT world.

The diversity of cultures, procedures, and performance requirements between IT computers and networks and SCADA systems are summarized in Table 4-1.

Table 4-1   IT versus SCADA System Performance Requirements

IT COMPUTERS & NETWORKS	SCADA SYSTEM
Data loss and interruptions can usually be tolerated through restoration from back-ups and restarts.	Data loss and interruptions cannot be tolerated and might result in serious consequences, including damage to equipment possible loss of life.
High data rates needed, delays can be accommodated.	Deterministic response times in local control loops; real-time responses needed; large delays or down-times cannot be tolerated.
Recovery accomplished by rebooting; system crashes and restarts do not usually have dangerous and life-threatening consequences.	Systems must usually be fault-tolerant or have hot back-ups; computer and controller crashes might result in dangerous and life-threatening situations.
Antivirus software widely employed.	Antivirus software difficult to employ in most instances because delays cannot be tolerated, excess computing capacity at the local controller might not be available, and determinism must be preserved.
Information-system security awareness and training reasonably high.	Low to moderate security awareness and training.

Table 4-1 *(continued)*

IT COMPUTERS & NETWORKS	SCADA SYSTEM
Encryption used.	Many SCADA systems transmit data and control messages in unencrypted form.
Penetration testing used routinely.	Penetration testing not routinely performed in the control network and, when performed, it must be done with care so as not to disrupt the control systems.
Implementation of software patches performed routinely.	Implementation of software patches must be carefully considered, performed infrequently, and usually requires cooperation with component vendors.
Information security audits required and routinely performed.	Information security audits not routinely performed.
Equipment usually replaced or upgraded every three to five years.	Equipment used for long periods of time without replacement.

At British Columbia Institute of Technology (BCIT), researchers found that reported attacks against SCADA systems have increased from 2 in 2001 to 10 reported incidents in 2003. As cause for further concern, BCIT researchers estimate that only 1 in 10 SCADA security incidents are reported. In most cases, organizations do not report attacks in order to avoid bad publicity and loss of confidence in their operations.

Eric Byres, a research faculty member in BCIT, attributes the increase in malicious incidents from external sources to the use of IT technologies and standards such as Microsoft Windows, Ethernet, Web Services, and interconnections between SCADA networks and the business IT environment.

The major risk elements to SCADA systems are summarized as follows:

- Connections to additional, possibly vulnerable networks
- Using standard hardware platforms with known vulnerabilities
- Using standard software with known vulnerabilities
- Other vulnerable remote connections
- Real-time deterministic requirements in contrast to information security controls that might cause delays

The accumulation of these elements and the resultant increased risk that has evolved over time is illustrated in Figure 4-1.

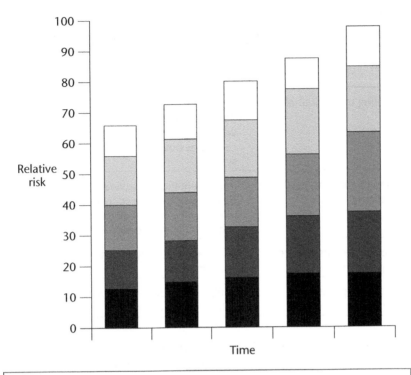

Figure 4-1   SCADA system evolving risk components

Managing Risk

Knowledge of the major SCADA system risk components can be applied in a risk management process for SCADA operations. The fundamental concepts of managing risk in the information security arena are well known and can be applied effectively to SCADA system security. This section reviews the basic risk management concepts used to reduce risk in SCADA systems.

Risk Management Components

Risk management is designed to reduce the negative impact of threats that materialize and exploit the vulnerabilities inherent in SCADA systems. Risk management involves assessing the risk, mitigating the risk, and then continuously evaluating system risks. The important definitions related to risk management are given in the following list:

- **Risk:** The probability that a specific threat will cause harm to a SCADA system by exploiting vulnerability in it

- **Threat:** An event that has the potential to negatively impact a SCADA system. A threat is directed against the confidentiality, integrity, or availability of a SCADA system.

- **Vulnerability:** A weakness in a SCADA system that could be exploited by a threat

- **Safeguard:** A countermeasure or security control designed to reduce the risk associated with a specific threat or group of threats

- **Impact:** The effect or consequence of a threat realized against a SCADA system

The following equation is often used to quantify the cost impact of a threat realized:

Annualized Loss Expectancy (ALE) = Single Loss Expectancy (SLE) × Annualized Rate of Occurrence (ARO)

In this equation, ALE is the annual value of the financial loss to an organization resulting from a threat realized, SLE is the value of the financial loss resulting from a single occurrence of a threat realized, and ARO is the estimated annual frequency of occurrence of the threat. The SLE is derived from the value of the asset impacted by the threat times an exposure factor (EF) that reflects the real exposure of the asset to the particular threat. The EF can take on values from 0 to 1. For example, if an asset has some protection from the threat realized and has a 50 percent chance of surviving the threat, it would have an EF of 0.5. Thus, if this asset had a value of $100,000 and the threat had a probability of occurring once every ten years, the ALE calculation would be

ALE = (Asset Value × EF) × ARO = ($100,000 × 0.5) x 1/10 = $5,000

Assessing the Risk

Risk assessment of a SCADA system comprises the steps summarized in Table 4-2.

Table 4-2   Risk Assessment Steps

STEP	FUNCTION
Characterization of the SCADA system	Define the scope of the SCADA risk assessment and gather information required for the process.
Identification of threats to the SCADA system	Determine and compile a list of the threats to the SCADA system.
Identification of vulnerabilities in the SCADA system	Analyze the vulnerabilities in the SCADA system that are susceptible to exploitation by the identified threats.
Analysis of the planned or in-place controls for the SCADA system	Determine and evaluate the extant or planned security controls aimed at protecting the SCADA system from threats that might exploit the SCADA system vulnerabilities.
Determination of the probability that a vulnerability in the SCADA system might be exploited by a threat	Rate the likelihood that a threat to the SCADA system will be successful in exploiting vulnerability in the system and causing harm.
Analysis of the impact of a threat realized against the SCADA system	Estimate the harmful impact that a threat realized would have on the SCADA system, based on the system criticality, the function of the system, and the degree of confidentiality of system data.
Determination of the level of risk that exists for the SCADA systems	Evaluate the risk to the system based on threats, vulnerabilities, and the adequacy of extant or planned SCADA system security controls.
Specification of SCADA security controls to be implemented in the risk mitigation process	Identify the SCADA system security controls that need to be implemented based on cost, effectiveness, and other related factors.
Documentation of the risk assessment process	Prepare a risk assessment report to provide the necessary information concerning the assessment decisions.

Mitigating the Risk

In risk assessment, the proper SCADA security controls are specified. The risk mitigation process implements these controls on a priority basis. The implementation of controls does not completely eliminate risk, but reduces the level of risk to an acceptable value. The controls can be technical, physical, or administrative. The risk that remains after the SCADA security controls are put in place is known as *residual risk*. Table 4-3 lists the different risk mitigation alternatives.

Table 4-3 Risk Mitigation Alternatives

ALTERNATIVES	DESCRIPTION
Risk transference	Transfer the risk to an outside organization, such as an insurance company.
Risk avoidance	Eliminate selected functions or services that have a high vulnerability from the SCADA systems.
Risk assumption	Recognize and understand the risk and continue operation.
Risk limitation	Use controls to limit the harmful impact of successful attacks.
Research and development	Conduct research into the various types of SCADA security controls.

SCADA Threats and Attack Routes

Typical threats to IT systems are also threats to SCADA systems if the threats have a means to exploit the vulnerabilities of SCADA systems.

Threats

Threats to SCADA systems can be the result of natural phenomena, malicious acts by individuals, accidents, improper procedures, or technical failures. Historically, threats to SCADA systems have been primarily from internal sources, including organization staff members, plant operators, or technical support personnel. Some examples of threats to SCADA system are listed here:

- Autonomous worms that randomly search for propagation paths
- Distributed-denial-of-service (DDoS) attacks, such as those that overwhelm the network bandwidth
- Viruses
- Trojan horses
- Human error
- Accidents
- Terrorists
- Disruption of utilities
- Noise on power lines

- Electromagnetic interference (EMI) and radio frequency interference (RFI)
- Plant shutdown for maintenance and start-up after maintenance (many harmful events occur as a result of plant maintenance shutdown and start-up)
- Improper application of software patches
- Interdependence with other networks and support elements
- Natural disasters such as earthquakes, tornadoes, volcanoes, fire, thunderstorms, and snow storms

SCADA Attack Routes

For a threat to be realized, it must have a means to access the SCADA system. Because SCADA systems typically now have connections with the Internet, corporate networks, and the public switched telephone network, there are a variety of paths into the SCADA control network. Additional paths to the control network are through satellite and wireless communication systems.

Some typical SCADA attack routes are listed here:

- Internet connections
- Business or enterprise network connections
- Connections to other networks that contain vulnerabilities
- Compromised virtual private networks (VPNs)
- Back-door connections through dial-up modems
- Unsecured wireless connections discovered by war-driving laptop users
- Malformed IP packets, in which packet header information conflicts with actual packet data
- IP fragmentation attacks, where a small fragment is transmitted that forces some of the TCP header field into a second fragment
- Through vulnerabilities in the simple network management protocol (SNMP), which is used to gather network information and provide notification of network events
- Open computer ports, such as UDP or TCP ports that are unprotected or left open unnecessarily
- Weak authentication in protocols and SCADA elements

- Maintenance hooks or trap doors, which are means to circumvent security controls during SCADA system development, testing, and maintenance

- E-mail transactions on control network

- Buffer overflow attacks on SCADA control servers, which are accessed by PLCs and SCADA human machine interfaces

- Leased, private telephone lines

Typical Attacker Privilege Goals

If an attacker were successful in penetrating a SCADA system, the next step would be to gain some level of control of the SCADA system components. The degree of control acquired is a function of the protections associated with each component, its visibility to the attacker, and the capabilities and intentions of the attacker.

Examples of exploitations that might be accomplished by a hacker through a malicious attack on a SCADA system are listed here:

- Obtain access to the SCADA system

- Obtain access to SCADA master control station

- Compromise the RTU or local PLCs

- Compromise the SCADA master control station

- Obtain SCADA system passwords from master control station

- Obtain access to RTUs or local PLCs

- Spoof RTU and send incorrect data to master control station

- Spoof master control station and send incorrect data to RTU

- Shut down the master control station

- Shut down local control RTUs

- Disrupt communications between SCADA master control station and RTUs

- Modify RTU control program

These actions and their relative harmful impact on a SCADA system are given in Figure 4-2. In the figure, impact is represented by a relative scale of 1 to 10, with 10 being the most severe.

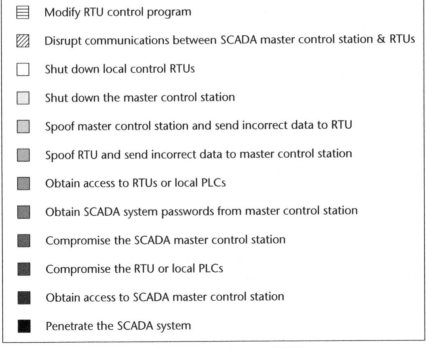

Figure 4-2   Relative impacts of malicious actions on SCADA systems

SCADA Honeynet Project

A novel approach to information system security, which has been applied to IT systems, is the *honeypot*. A honeypot is a decoy in an IT system that is used to lure a hacker away from critical resources. The honeypot is monitored to gain information about the attacker, such as the type of attack being initiated and the attacker's characteristics. Lance Spitzner, president of the Honeynet Project, defines a honeypot as "an information system resource whose value lies in unauthorized or illicit use of that resource." The Honeynet Project is a nonprofit research organization of volunteer security professionals dedicated to advancing the state of the art in information system security. A *honeynet* is a controlled network of high-interaction honeypots that are presented as decoys to monitor and gain information about network attackers.

Honeypots and honeynets are currently being explored for use in protecting SCADA systems. As a prelude to the SCADA system security honeynet discussion, it is useful to review some of the basic definitions relating to honeypots and honeynets.

Honeypots

In enterprise networks, honeypots are used to deter attackers from critical targets, detect ongoing attacks, obtain detailed attack data, and respond to attacks. Honeypots can also be used in a research mode to identify new threats and hacking approaches. Honeypots can be taken off-line to review data and are also able to process encrypted information.

Honeypots can be described as either high-interaction or low-interaction. A *high-interaction* honeypot has the ability to interact more realistically with an attacker because it employs operating systems and associated services. It has the ability to gather significant amounts of data about the attacker, but is more prone to penetration because it does use popular operating systems and software.

A *low-interaction* honeypot provides a partial simulation of an operating system and associated services. This type of honeypot is less complex than a high-interaction honeypot and is easier to deploy. However, because it is a limited simulation, it is easier for an attacker to discern that it is a honeypot and not a real operating system. Yet, this situation makes it more difficult for an intruder to compromise the honeypot and use it for malicious purposes against other computers.

An example of a low-interaction honeypot is Honeyd, an open source honeypot developed by Niels Provos, (www.honeyd.org/). Provos states "Honeyd is a small daemon that runs both on UNIX-like and Windows platforms." Honeyd can be used to spawn a number of virtual honeypots on a computer and provide a range of system services such as HTTP and FTP. It can also be used to support the simulation of larger networks. In operation, Honeyd simulates TCP/IP stacks and applications, monitors connections to ports such as UDP and TCP, keeps track of attackers' actions, and acquires information on passwords, IDs, and other messages sent by an attacker. In monitoring port connections, Honeyd can run a script on a specific port that provides a signature of a SCADA component whenever someone connects to that port.

An organization using honeypots has to be cautious, because legal and liability issues are involved. Possibly prosecutable issues include the violation of privacy rights of individuals when monitoring their activities, when a honeypot of one organization is used to attack another organization's computers, storing of illegal or stolen information on a honeypot, and entrapment.

Honeynet Project

The Honeynet project was begun in 1999 as a research activity to evaluate and explore the use of honeypots and honeynets to increase the knowledge of attackers' behaviors, motivation, attack tools, and other relevant information. The project began with 30 members and, in 2002, established the Honeynet Research Alliance, which comprises volunteer members from around the world, including Greece, Spain, Brazil, India, and Ireland. In Phase 1 of the Honeynet project, from 1999 to 2002, the research efforts focused on proof of concept honeynets. Phase 2, from 2002 to 2003, focused on developing second-generation (GenII) standards and improved honeypot capabilities, including the ability to process encrypted information. Phase 3, which was conducted from 2003 to 2004, produced production versions of the GenII honeypot technologies and made them available on CD-ROM for deployment. Phase 4 began in 2004 and emphasizes central data collection and analysis from distributed honeynets and user-friendly human machine interfaces.

SCADA Honeynet

The goal of the SCADA Honeynet Project is to evaluate the feasibility of simulating industrial networks, including SCADA systems, PLC architectures, distributed control systems, and their associated protocols. The project, which is sponsored by the Cisco Critical Infrastructure Protection Group (CIAG), comprises requirements analysis and documentation, development of proof-of-concept software in the form of Honeyd scripts, and release of the code for evaluation purposes. The scripts are designed to support the simulation of SCADA-system elements in various network architectures. The next step will be to use the SCADA honeypots to gather information about attackers and their approaches, similar to the information obtained when deploying honeypots in non-SCADA applications. Then, countermeasures will be designed to mitigate attacks against SCADA systems.

Venkat Pothamsetty and Matthew Franz, of the CIAG SCADA Honeynet Project, have identified the following functionality as required to properly simulate SCADA system components to attackers attempting to compromise the SCADA system:

- Simulation of the TCP/IP stack of Ethernet-based SCADA components that might be scanned with detection tools such as Xprobe and Nmap

- Simulation of a wide variety of SCADA protocols

- Simulation of SCADA device applications

- Simulation of SCADA physical layer interfaces such as EIA-232 and EIA-485

- Simulation of the entry point of a router that separates the plant control network router from the corporate or enterprise network, including wireless routers or wireless bridges

- Simulation of a modem connected to a local control device, such as a PLC

- Simulation of Ethernet-connected control elements

- Simulation of SCADA human machine interfaces

A problem with simulating SCADA systems is that, unlike IT systems, there is not a large database of SCADA vulnerabilities or security advisories from which to build realistic scenarios of attacks and possible consequences of those attacks.

Summary

Industry associations, information security professionals, control engineers, managers, and a cadre of government and private officials are recognizing the importance of protecting SCADA systems. This recognition is not as widespread as it should be at this time, but it is growing. From believing that SCADA systems were invulnerable or, at least, not of interest to anyone with malicious intent, the SCADA community is developing security standards, conducting training, and focusing on best practices and safeguards for securing SCADA systems. The same risk management and vulnerability analysis techniques that have been standard practice for IT systems are now being applied to SCADA systems and their associated networks and control components. The industry is categorizing the threats to SCADA operations and developing guidelines and methodologies for improving their security posture.

SCADA Security Methods and Techniques

Although some aspects of SCADA systems are amenable to IT system security techniques, other critical portions of SCADA implementations might be limited and degraded by the application of these techniques. This situation is particularly true when the security hardware or software consume SCADA system resources to the extent that deterministic performance and responses are degraded and key functions are not properly executed.

This chapter examines information-system security best practices and methods and how they can be adapted to operate effectively in a SCADA environment.

SCADA Security Mechanisms

There are security mechanisms that can improve the security posture of SCADA systems. Many of these approaches parallel those used in IT security but have to be applied in accordance with SCADA performance and criticality requirements. As in conventional information-system security implementations, SCADA security mechanisms fall into the categories of physical, administrative, and technical controls.

Improving Cybersecurity of SCADA Networks

In September 2002, the President's Critical Infrastructure Protection Board and the U.S. Department of Energy issued a document entitled *21 Steps to Improve Cyber Security of SCADA Networks*. This document provides a list of information-system security actions and procedures geared to the needs and characteristics of SCADA systems. The 21 steps are listed as follows and summarized graphically in Figure 5-1:

1. Identify all connections to SCADA networks. Conduct a thorough risk analysis to assess the risk and necessity of each connection to the SCADA network. Develop a comprehensive understanding of all connections to the SCADA network, and how well these connections are protected. Identify and evaluate the following types of connections:

- Internal local area and wide area networks, including business networks
- The Internet
- Wireless network devices, including satellite uplinks
- Modem or dial-up connections
- Connections to business partners, vendors, or regulatory agencies

2. Disconnect unnecessary connections to the SCADA network. To ensure the highest degree of security of SCADA systems, isolate the SCADA network from other network connections as much as possible. Any connection to another network introduces security risks, particularly if the connection creates a pathway from or to the Internet. Although direct connections with other networks may allow important information to be passed efficiently and conveniently, insecure connections are simply not worth the risk; isolation of the SCADA network must be a primary goal to provide needed protection. Strategies such as using demilitarized zones (DMZs) and data warehousing can facilitate the secure transfer of data from the SCADA network to business networks. However, strategies must be designed and implemented properly to avoid introduction of additional risk through improper configuration.

3. Evaluate and strengthen the security of any remaining connections to the SCADA network. Conduct penetration testing or vulnerability analysis of any remaining connections to the SCADA network to evaluate the protection posture associated with these pathways. Use this information in conjunction with risk management processes to develop a robust protection strategy for any pathways to the SCADA network. Because the SCADA network is only as secure as its weakest connecting point, it is essential to implement firewalls, intrusion detection systems (IDSs), and other appropriate security measures at each point of entry. Configure firewall rules to prohibit access from and to the SCADA network, and be as specific as possible when permitting approved connections. For example, an independent system operator (ISO) should not be granted blanket network access simply because there is a need for a connection to certain components of the SCADA system. Strategically place IDSs at each entry point to alert security personnel of potential breaches of network security. Organization management must understand and accept responsibility for risks associated with any connection to the SCADA network.

4. *Harden SCADA networks by removing or disabling unnecessary services.* SCADA control servers built on commercial or open-source operating systems can be exposed to attack through default network services. To the greatest degree possible, remove or disable unused services and network daemons to reduce the risk of direct attack. This is particularly important when SCADA networks are interconnected with other networks. Do not permit a service or feature on a SCADA network unless a thorough risk assessment of the consequences of allowing the service or feature shows that its benefits far outweigh the potential for vulnerability exploitation. Examples of services to remove from SCADA networks include automated meter reading and remote billing systems, e-mail services, and Internet access. An example of a feature to disable is remote maintenance. Numerous secure configuration guidelines, such as the National Security Agency's series of security guides, for both commercial and open-source operating systems, are in the public domain. Additionally, work closely with SCADA vendors to identify secure configurations and coordinate all changes to operational systems to ensure that removing or disabling services does not cause downtime, interruption of service, or loss of support.

5. *Do not rely on proprietary protocols to protect your system.* Some SCADA systems use unique, proprietary protocols for communications between field devices and servers. Often the security of SCADA systems is based solely on the secrecy of these protocols. Unfortunately, obscure protocols provide very little real security. Do not rely on proprietary protocols or factory-default configuration settings to protect your system. Additionally, demand that vendors disclose any back doors or vendor interfaces to your SCADA systems, and expect them to provide systems that are capable of being secured.

6. *Implement the security features provided by device and system vendors.* Older SCADA systems (most systems in use) have no security features whatsoever. SCADA system owners must insist that their system vendor implement security features in the form of product patches or upgrades. Some newer SCADA devices are shipped with basic security features, but these are usually disabled to ensure ease of installation. Analyze each SCADA device to determine whether security features are present. Additionally, factory-default security settings (such as in computer network firewalls) are often set to provide maximum usability, but minimal security. Set all security features to provide the maximum level of security. Allow settings below maximum security only after performing a thorough risk assessment of the consequences of reducing the security level.

7. Establish strong controls over any medium that is used as a backdoor into the SCADA network. Where backdoors or vendor connections do exist in SCADA systems, strong authentication must be implemented to ensure secure communications. Modems, wireless, and wired networks used for communications and maintenance represent a significant vulnerability to the SCADA network and remote sites. Successful war-dialing or war-driving attacks could allow an attacker to bypass all other controls and have direct access to the SCADA network or resources. To minimize the risk of such attacks, disable inbound access and replace it with some type of callback system.

8. Implement internal and external intrusion detection systems and establish 24-hour-a-day incident monitoring. To be able to effectively respond to cyberattacks, establish an intrusion detection strategy that includes alerting network administrators of malicious network activity originating from internal or external sources. Intrusion detection system monitoring is essential 24 hours a day; this capability can be easily set up through a pager. Additionally, incident response procedures must be in place to allow an effective response to any attack. To complement network monitoring, enable logging on all systems and audit system logs daily to detect suspicious activity as soon as possible.

9. Perform technical audits of SCADA devices and networks, and any other connected networks, to identify security concerns. Technical audits of SCADA devices and networks are critical to ongoing security effectiveness. Many commercial and open-source security tools are available that allow system administrators to conduct audits of their systems and networks to identify active services, patch level, and common vulnerabilities. These tools will not solve systemic problems, but they will eliminate the paths of least resistance that an attacker could exploit. Analyze identified vulnerabilities to determine their significance, and take corrective actions as appropriate. Track corrective actions and analyze this information to identify trends. Additionally, retest systems after corrective actions have been taken to ensure that vulnerabilities were actually eliminated. Scan nonproduction environments actively to identify and address potential problems.

10. Conduct physical security surveys and assess all remote sites connected to the SCADA network to evaluate their security. Any location that has a connection to the SCADA network is a target, especially unmanned or unguarded remote sites. Conduct a physical security survey and inventory access points at each facility that has a connection to the SCADA system. Identify and assess any source of information, including remote cables (telephone, computer network, fiber optic, and so on) that could be tapped; radio and microwave links that are exploitable; computer terminals that could be accessed; and wireless local area network access points. Identify and eliminate single points of failure. The security of the site must be adequate to detect or prevent unauthorized access. Do not allow live network access points at remote, unguarded sites simply for convenience.

11. Establish SCADA Red Teams to identify and evaluate possible attack scenarios. Establish a Red Team to identify potential attack scenarios and evaluate potential system vulnerabilities. (A *Red Team* is a group of experts who provide independent evaluations of projects, proposals, approaches, and so on, so that weaknesses can be corrected.) Use a variety of people who can provide insight into weaknesses of the overall network, SCADA systems, physical systems, and security controls. People who work on the system every day have great insight into the vulnerabilities of your SCADA network and should be consulted when identifying potential attack scenarios and possible consequences. Also, ensure that the risk from a malicious insider is fully evaluated, given that this represents one of the greatest threats to an organization. Feed information resulting from the Red Team evaluation into risk management processes to assess the information and establish appropriate protection strategies.

12. Clearly define cybersecurity roles, responsibilities, and authorities for managers, system administrators, and users. Organization personnel need to understand the specific expectations associated with protecting information technology resources through the definition of clear and logical roles and responsibilities. In addition, key personnel need to be given sufficient authority to carry out their assigned responsibilities. Too often, good cybersecurity is left up to individual initiative, which usually leads to inconsistent implementations and ineffective security. Establish a cybersecurity structure in the organization that defines roles and responsibilities and clearly identifies how cybersecurity issues are escalated and who is notified in an emergency.

13. Document network architecture and identify systems that serve critical functions or contain sensitive information that require additional levels of protection. Develop and document robust information security architecture as part of a process to establish an effective protection strategy. It is essential that organizations design their networks with security in mind and continue to have a strong understanding of their network architecture throughout its lifecycle. Of particular importance is an in-depth understanding of the functions that the systems perform and the sensitivity of the stored information. Without this understanding, risk cannot be properly assessed and protection strategies may not be sufficient. Documenting the information security architecture and its components is critical to understanding the overall protection strategy and identifying single points of failure.

14. Establish a rigorous, ongoing risk management process. A thorough understanding of the risks to network computing resources from denial-of-service attacks and the vulnerability of sensitive information to compromise is essential to an effective cybersecurity program. Risk assessments form the technical basis of this understanding and are critical to formulating effective strategies to mitigate vulnerabilities and preserve the integrity of computing resources. Initially, perform a baseline risk analysis based on a current threat assessment to use for developing a network protection strategy. Due to rapidly changing technology and the emergence of new threats on a daily basis, an ongoing risk assessment process is also needed so that routine changes can be made to the protection strategy to ensure it remains effective. Fundamental to risk management are identification of residual risk with a network protection strategy in place and acceptance of that risk by management.

15. Establish a network protection strategy based on the principle of defense-in-depth. A fundamental principle that must be part of any network protection strategy is *defense-in-depth.* Defense-in-depth must be considered early in the design phase of the development process, and must be an integral consideration in all technical decision making associated with the network. Use technical and administrative controls to mitigate threats from identified risks to as great a degree as possible at all levels of the network. Single points of failure must be avoided, and cybersecurity defense must be layered to limit and contain the impact of any security incidents. Additionally, each layer must be protected against other systems at the same layer. For example, to protect against the insider threat, restrict users to access only those resources necessary to perform their job functions.

16. Clearly identify cybersecurity requirements. Organizations and companies need structured security programs with mandated requirements to establish expectations and allow personnel to be held accountable. Formalized policies and procedures are typically used to establish and institutionalize a cybersecurity program. A formal program is essential for establishing a consistent, standards-based approach to cybersecurity throughout an organization and eliminating sole dependence on individual initiative. Policies and procedures also inform employees of their specific cybersecurity responsibilities and the consequences of failing to meet those responsibilities. They also provide guidance regarding actions to be taken during a cybersecurity incident and promote efficient and effective actions during a time of crisis. As part of identifying cybersecurity requirements, include user agreements, notifications, and warning banners. Establish requirements to minimize the threat from malicious insiders, including conducting background checks and limiting network privileges only to those who need it.

17. Establish effective configuration management processes. A fundamental management process needed to maintain a secure network is configuration management. Configuration management needs to cover both hardware configurations and software configurations. Changes to hardware or software can easily introduce vulnerabilities that undermine network security. Processes are required to evaluate and control any change to ensure that the network remains secure. Configuration management begins with well-tested and documented security baselines for your various systems.

18. Conduct routine self-assessments. Robust performance evaluation processes are needed to provide organizations with feedback on the effectiveness of cybersecurity policy and technical implementation. A sign of a mature organization is one that is able to identify its own issues, conduct root-cause analyses, and implement effective corrective actions that address individual and systemic problems. Self-assessment processes that are normally part of an effective cyber-security program include routine scanning for vulnerabilities, automated audit-ing of the network, and self-assessments of organizational and individual performance.

19. Establish system backups and disaster recovery plans. Establish a disaster recovery plan that allows rapid recovery from any emergency (including a cyberattack). System backups are an essential part of any plan and allow rapid reconstruction of the network. Routinely exercise disaster recovery plans to ensure that they work and that personnel are familiar with them. Make appropriate changes to disaster recovery plans based on lessons learned from exercises.

20. Senior organizational leadership should establish expectations for cybersecurity performance and hold individuals accountable for their performance. Effective cyber-security performance requires commitment and leadership from senior man-agers in the organization. It is essential that senior management establish an expectation for strong cybersecurity and that they communicate this expecta-tion to their subordinate managers throughout the organization. It is also essential that senior organizational leadership establish a structure to imple-ment the cybersecurity program. This structure will promote consistent imple-mentation and sustained strength in the cybersecurity program. It is then important for individuals to be held accountable for their performance as it relates to cybersecurity. This includes managers, system administrators, tech-nicians, and users/operators.

21. Establish policies and conduct training to minimize the likelihood that organi-zational personnel will inadvertently disclose sensitive information regarding SCADA system design, operations, or security controls. Release data related to the SCADA network only on a strict, need-to-know basis, and only to persons explicitly authorized to receive such information. Social engineering, the gath-ering of information about a computer or computer network via questions to naive users, is often the first step in a malicious attack on computer networks. The more information revealed about a computer or computer network, the more vulnerable the computer or network is. Never divulge data related to a SCADA network, including the names and contact information of the system operators and administrators, computer operating systems, and the physical and logical locations of computers and network systems over telephones or to personnel unless they are explicitly authorized to receive such information. Any requests for information by unknown persons need to be sent to a central network security location for verification and fulfillment. People can be a weak link in an otherwise secure network. Conduct training and information awareness campaigns to ensure that personnel remain diligent in guarding sensitive network information, particularly their passwords.

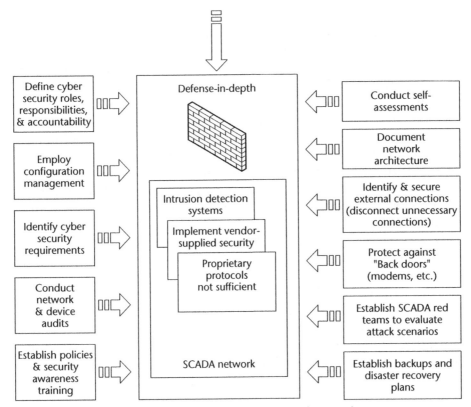

Figure 5-1   Graphical summary of 21 steps of SCADA cybersecurity.

Implementing Security Improvements

The 21 steps can be implemented in a variety of ways, subject to the network architecture and type of SCADA application. Some examples of applying the 21 steps are summarized as follows:

- Isolate the SCADA network using encryption, strong authentication, segmented network topologies, biometrics, and by disconnecting the network from unnecessary external connections.

- Conduct vulnerability analyses on the network and its nodes.

- Perform a risk assessment on the network and each connection point to the enterprise network.

- Develop and implement an incident response and remediation plan.

- Remove or disable all unnecessary services.

- Apply firewalls that are compatible with requirements of SCADA systems:

  - Existing firewalls are not aware of SCADA protocols such as Foundation fieldbus and Modbus and cannot filter on content of such protocols.

  - Local control units at the facility under control are usually more vulnerable than the central control facility. Again, firewalls at field locations can use access control lists for some protection, but vulnerabilities still exist to most common types of attacks.

  - Many of today's SCADA systems employ an organization's enterprise wide area network to facilitate the exchange of data between the field sites and the central control location. Also, the enterprise network is usually connected to the Internet. If a filtering firewall is not properly implemented between the SCADA system and the enterprise network, both the central control servers and the PLCs and RTUs at the remote sites are susceptible to attacks such as spoofing, viruses, and denial of service.

- Install and operate intrusion detection systems.

- Provide for backup of critical software and data.

- Apply configuration management to SCADA and network software and hardware.

- Incorporate patch management to SCADA and network software and hardware.

- Conduct security audits.

- Implement an enterprise-wide security awareness program, including handouts, slogans, login banners, briefings, and training classes.

- Develop and test business continuity and disaster recovery plans.

These security mechanisms, implemented with recognition of the special needs and characteristics of SCADA systems, will significantly improve the security posture of real-time data acquisition and control systems and allow these systems to perform their designated critical functions and operations.

SCADA Intrusion Detection Systems

An intrusion detection system (IDS) comprises hardware or software or a combination of these that are designed to monitor and analyze activities on a host computer or a network in order to determine if a malicious event has occurred or is occurring. A malicious event is any activity that is intended to compromise the confidentiality, integrity, or availability of the host computer or network. In addition to detecting an attack, an IDS is particularly useful in detecting precursors to an attack, such as scans and probes that search for open ports or other means of entry into a computer or network.

IDSs are also useful in characterizing threats against computers or networks because they collect information prior to, during, and after an attack or attack attempt. This record of information is useful if the targeted organization wishes to pursue legal avenues against the intruder.

In applying an IDS, the acquired data should be stored and analyzed in a location separate from the environment under surveillance.

Types of Intrusion Detection Systems

IDSs can be characterized by their location and source of data to be collected and analyzed, by the means of analyzing the data, and by the response taken to detected intrusions. The main types of IDSs based on the location and source of data collected are network-based and host-based IDSs. Signature-based and anomaly-based IDSs are distinguished by their methods of analyzing suspected attack information. IDSs characterized by response are designated as active-response, passive-response, or hybrid-response mechanisms, the latter using a combination of active and passive response approaches.

Network-Based and Host-Based IDS

A network-based IDS captures and evaluates message packets traveling over a network segment. These IDSs are typically passive devices that use sensors to monitor network traffic and are designed to protect the host computers. In times of high network traffic, a network-based IDS might experience problems in monitoring all the packets and might miss an attack being launched. Also, a network-based IDS cannot analyze encrypted packets and, therefore, cannot identify an attack using encrypted messages. A third weakness of a network-based IDS is that, even though it can tell whether an attack was launched, it cannot determine the result of the attack. Thus, manual intervention is required to discern if the attack was successful against a network host.

A host-based IDS monitors and analyzes information on a specific host computer. As a result, it can provide more details on the attack and the entities affected as well as determine the outcome of the attack. Because this type of IDS resides on a host computer, it can also access information before it is encrypted or after it is decrypted, allowing it, in many instances, to gather attack information when data is transmitted in encrypted form. In order to analyze potential attacks, a host-based IDS uses information from system logs and operating system audit trails. Many of the advantages of a host-based IDS are the result of the IDS residing on the host, but this characteristic also consumes a host's computing resources and makes the IDS vulnerable to direct attacks such as denial of service.

A subset of the host-based IDS type is an application-based IDS. It has the characteristics of a host-based IDS and evaluates operations in a software application. Consequently, it can monitor for attacks between the user and application, such as users attempting to access data beyond their clearance level.

Signature-Based and Anomaly-Based IDS

A signature-based IDS, or misuse IDS as it is sometimes called, monitors system activity and compares the activity characteristics with characteristics or patterns of known attacks stored in a database. Because this type of IDS bases its alarms on matching a known attack pattern, it can provide specific information on the type of attack and generates less false positives than an anomaly-based IDS. A disadvantage of a signature-based IDS is that it cannot detect new attack types that are not stored in the attack signature database. Therefore, the database must constantly be updated with patterns of new attacks. Also, in applying a signature-based IDS to SCADA, the attack signature database will have different characteristics than signatures in an IT-oriented database. In particular, the signatures will have to be correlated with SCADA protocols such as Foundation fieldbus, Modbus, Profinet, ControlNet, and so on. Typical SCADA IDS signature components include IP addresses, transmitted parameters, and protocols.

An anomaly-based IDS takes statistical samples of network or host operating information to develop a profile of normal activities on a system. Then, when these network or host statistics deviate from the norm, it usually indicates that an attack is in progress. Statistics used to characterize normal behavior include CPU utilization rate and the number of failed login attempts. An advantage of this type of IDS is that it can detect new attacks, but it can also be deceived by attacks that do not significantly change the parameters being measured. In addition, an anomaly-based IDS can generate false alarms if legitimate activity on the host or network causes the statistical parameters to change enough to trigger an attack alarm.

Active-Response IDS

An active-response IDS takes some form of action in the event of an intrusion. The typical available responses are summarized in the following list:

- Explore the environment and acquire additional information that would be relevant in identifying an attack.

- Block network ports and protocols used by the suspected attacker.

- Change router and firewall access lists to block messages from the suspected attacker's IP address.

Passive-Response IDS

A passive response IDS provides information about an attack to an individual who can, subsequently, decide on the proper course of action. The individual can be notified in the form of a call to a cell phone or pager, an e-mail message, an alert on a computer terminal screen, or a message to a simple network management protocol (SNMP) console. The information provided by the alert can include the following:

- The source IP address of the attack

- The IP address of the target of the attack

- The result of the attack

- The tool or mechanism used to launch the attack

- Reports and logs of system attacks and relevant events

Processing of IDS Data

IDSs can collect and analyze data on possible intrusions continually as the data is acquired or in block form after an event has occurred. In the continuous mode, also known as real-time processing, the data is analyzed as it is collected, thus providing the user with the opportunity to take action while the intrusion is in progress. Analyzing the IDS information in block form after an intrusion has taken place is called *batch-mode* or *interval-based* processing. In this case, the user cannot intervene during an event. Batch-mode was common in early IDS implementations because their capabilities did not support real-time data acquisition and analysis.

Vulnerability Scanning and Analysis

Vulnerability analysis is a host-based, batch-mode IDS that gathers data to determine vulnerabilities of a computer system or network. A vulnerability scan conducted by an organization to evaluate the security of its systems is known as ethical hacking. Scans are also conducted by attackers to gather information on a target system to facilitate a later attack on the system. Typical information that can be garnered by a vulnerability scan includes the following:

- Domain names and IP addresses
- Firewalls and perimeter devices
- General network infrastructure
- Intrusion detection systems
- Platforms and protocols
- Open ports
- Unauthorized software
- Running services

Friendly vulnerability scans should be conducted by a security professional with authorization from higher-level management. Even a friendly scan with good intentions has the potential to inadvertently cause damage to files and other critical processes running on the scanned system or network. A vulnerability scan and analysis should be conducted periodically to identify weaknesses in SCADA systems. Some typical scan types are listed here:

- **Discovery scanning:** Acquires information about network devices, including the type of device, services running, operating system used, and available ports.

- **Workstation scanning:** Gathers data on the corporate desktop configurations, including hardware and software, upgrades, and security patches.

- **Server scanning:** Determines server operating system configuration and identifies running applications, software versions, security patches, default accounts, weak passwords, and unauthorized programs.

- **Port scanning or probe:** Sends data packets to ports to acquire port information, including TCP and UDP ports in use, active hosts, operating-system type and release version, available network services, and remote logon capability.

A number of scanning tools are available for use by ethical hackers or malicious attackers. These tools include the following:

- **Computer Oracle and Password System (COPS):** Analyzes and reports known weaknesses in Unix systems.

- **System Administrator Tool for Analyzing Networks (SATAN):** Scans networked systems for known vulnerabilities.

- **Remote Access Perimeter Scanner (RAPS):** Detects most commercial remote-control and back-door packages; it is a professional version of PC Anywhere.
- **Nessus:** Audits the security state of Unix and Linux systems
- **NMap:** Scans most ports from numbers 1 to 1024, as well as a number of others in the registered and undefined ranges. NMap supports TCP and UDP port scans.
- **Tcpview:** Analyzes security issues associated with network services such as Finger, NFS, NIS, FTP, and TFTP.

SCADA Audit Logs

SCADA systems and their security components, by their very nature, continuously acquire and log data on nearly all aspects of a plant under control. These logs are a source of valuable information on the operations in the plant, including information on individuals attempting to access the system, data relating to attacks and attempted attacks, characterizations of port scans, and possible back-door entries into the SCADA system.

Examples of sources of important information are firewall audit logs, router audit logs, control server logs, web server logs, and logs associated with data switches.

Table 5-1 provides examples of how audit logs can be used to detect attacks on SCADA systems.

Table 5-1 Audit Logs Applied to Attack Detection and Analysis

IDS APPLICATION	DETECTION FUNCTION
Network-based IDS connected to the SCADA central control center to monitor the human machine interface, web servers, and connections to other enterprise networks	Monitors operating system audit logs for central servers, Web servers, and other principal systems.
Network-based IDS monitoring the DMZ and reading attack information from firewall logs and server logs	Detects attack at DMZ and determines outcome of attack.

Table 5-1   *(continued)*

IDS APPLICATION	DETECTION FUNCTION
Network-based IDS monitoring firewall logs	Detects attack at firewall.
Network-based IDS monitoring scanning and probes by potential attacker	Detects scans and thwarts attacker.
Network-based IDS monitoring control servers and control server logs for buffer overflow or denial of service attacks	Detects buffer overflow or denial-of-service attacks and consequences of attacks.
Host-based IDS residing on control software in host	Detects attacks on server host from server audit logs, but adds overhead to processing and might pose problems with response times of SCADA systems.

As noted in the last row of Table 5-1, host-based IDSs should be used with caution on control servers because of the added processing required. This additional use of a server's computational resources could affect the performance of the control server and cause delays in response times of the SCADA system.

Because IDSs are designed for IT systems, they do not take into consideration the protocols used in SCADA systems. However, because SCADA systems inherently log large amounts of information from various inputs, these records can provide input into an IDS to assist in detecting an attack and its consequences. For example, logged information such as the number of failed login attempts above a threshold or clipping level, modification of control points or alarm settings, and an increase in operator privileges might alert an IDS to a possible attack. Figure 5-2 illustrates some typical sources of audit logs that support the detection and analysis of attacks on SCADA systems.

In addition to the aforementioned audit logs, there are additional audit files that can be useful in both IT and SCADA applications. These logs are summarized in Table 5-2.

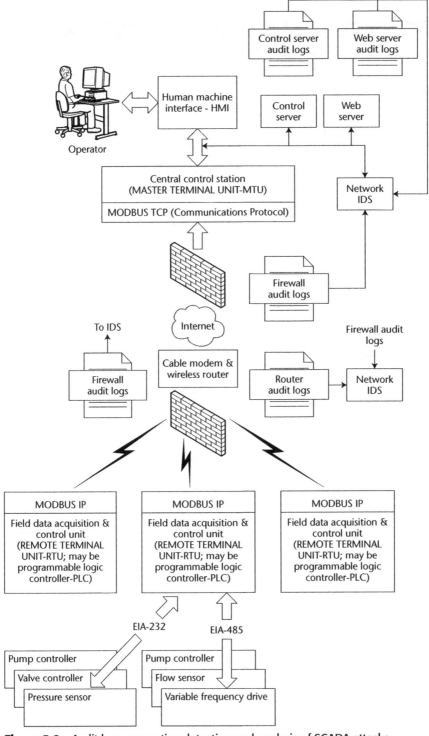

Figure 5-2 Audit logs supporting detection and analysis of SCADA attacks

Table 5-2 Additional Useful Log Files

FILE TYPE	INFORMATION PROVIDED
Resource utilization	Provides information on the level of utilization for all system resources.
Central processing unit (CPU)	Provides information on the usage and capacity of the CPU. Unusual changes in CPU utilization might indicate an attack or unauthorized access.
Invalid file access attempts	Indicates denial of attempted access to files.
Disk capacity	Provides an accounting of total disk capacity, disk capacity being used, and disk capacity available. Analysis can show possible unallocated disk sectors that might contain malicious code.
Memory consumption	Provides an accounting of total memory capacity and memory capacity being used. Analysis can reveal possible malicious processes.
System shutdown	Indicates when system operation was terminated, how it was terminated, and by whom it was terminated. This shutdown might allow an attacker to access files upon startup and bypass security mechanisms.
Process initiation	Provides information on the time a specific program was started and the associated user. This data is useful in analyzing programs launched by unauthorized individuals or processes.

Because log files contain critical information that is extremely useful in forensic analysis of attacks and attack attempts, they should be protected at the highest level of security available. Some effective methods of protecting audit log files include encryption, checksums, and digital signatures. A *checksum* performs a computation on the data to be protected and appends the result to the data. If the data is modified, a recalculation of the checksum using the same algorithm will yield a result different from the original checksum. A comparison of the two checksums will indicate if the data was changed from the original version. Similarly, a *digital signature* generates a message digest, similar to a checksum, using a one-way algorithm called a *hash function*. The message digest is appended to the data. If the original data is modified in any way, a recalculation of the message digest will yield a result different form the original message digest.

Security Awareness

Control engineers traditionally have been concerned with designing, developing, installing, operating, and maintaining effective, reliable, and safe control systems for a variety of domains. Technicians and plant operators are also involved, to some extent, in these various phases of control system applications. Historically, the predominant security measures were focused on physical security and some technical security to protect against malicious intent or accidents of insiders. The use of standard operating systems, hardware platforms, protocols, and connections to external networks now require a new level of awareness for control system personnel. A paradigm shift in thinking is required to address issues such as attacks through the organization's enterprise network, attacks through the Internet, the types of threats, SCADA system vulnerabilities, incident response, application of SCADA security standards, firewall management, disaster recovery, and risk management. In order to raise security awareness, employees have to be informed and educated about various security topics including the following:

- Their responsibilities relative to SCADA system security
- The organization's information system/SCADA security policy
- How to determine if an incident has occurred or is occurring
- What to do if an incident is discovered
- The reporting structure
- General consciousness of maintaining a proper security environment.

An important factor in security awareness training is to make sure that all employees participate equally in the program. In many instances, outside contractors, part-time employees, and night-shift employees miss out on training and awareness programs given to the full-time, day employees.

For security awareness to be successful, a useful tool is a security awareness plan. The plan does not have to be long and involved, but should simply cover the program's objectives, action items and dates, personnel assignments, and means to measure the progress of the program.

An effective measure to reinforce security awareness is to ensure that there are consequences to any individual who is in violation of an organization's security policy and security requirements. Punishments can range from warnings to dismissal, according to the severity of the violation. In addition, standard reminders and memory aids such as posters, logon banners, signs, videos, newsletters, and so on should be used to keep the topic of security in front of employees during their everyday activities.

Several critical conditions and practices should be in place for an organization to have a successful security awareness program. These include an information-system security policy, security-program goals, targeted personnel profiles, visible management support, and the use of motivational methods.

Formal training should be provided, commensurate with the roles and responsibilities of the affected personnel. For example, SCADA system operators and related plant personnel should be given detailed technical training in the components related to their areas of responsibility, while management personnel should be trained in higher-level general security issues.

As in any endeavor, metrics have to be developed and applied to gauge the effectiveness of a program. For security awareness, measures of knowledge acquired by the targeted personnel can be obtained through questionnaires, interviews, problem exercises, and question-and-answer sessions. In fact, one can obtain a good indication of the security awareness in an organization by asking relevant personnel some of the simple questions shown in Figure 5-3. The answers provided to these questions will reveal if security awareness has migrated throughout the organization to the extent that security threats can be handled in an appropriate manner.

Has your training prepared you to handle a security incident?

Would you recognize a security incident if it occurred?

Can you show me your copy of the security policy?

What does security awareness mean?

Would you feel comfortable in handling a security incident?

Does your organization have a security policy?

To whom would you report a suspected security incident?

What action would you take if you thought a security incident has occurred?

How often do you receive security awareness training or refresher briefings?

Figure 5-3   Security awareness questions

Summary

SCADA systems can be effectively protected against attacks and intrusions if conventional information-system security methods are modified and applied taking into account the demanding SCADA system performance and reliability requirements. Developing and applying SCADA-system security policies, eliminating unnecessary network connections and services, performing vulnerability analyses, relying on technical audits, managing risk, and providing security awareness training are basic proven approaches that will work in fortifying SCADA systems. IDSs are also important tools that can be applied successfully to detect and thwart intrusions into SCADA systems, but existing IDSs have to be altered to incorporate SCADA protocols and signature components.

CHAPTER 6

SCADA Security Standards and Reference Documents

The control engineering community, related organizational management, and governmental security organizations are becoming increasingly aware of the threats posed to SCADA systems either by malicious intent or accidents. Consequently, new SCADA security guidelines are being developed and existing information security standards and guidelines are being adapted to SCADA applications. In many cases, these new and revised guides build on information security principles that have been used for years in the IT environment. This chapter reviews some of the principal information security guidelines and standards that apply to SCADA systems. The guidelines covered are the British Standard (BS) for Information Security Management; the Instrumentation, Systems, and Automation Society (ISA) technical report *Security Technologies for Manufacturing and Control Systems*; the ISA technical report *Integrating Electronic Security into the Manufacturing and Control Systems Environment*,; Government Accountability Office (GAO) document GAO-04-140T, *Critical Infrastructure Protection, Challenges in Securing Control Systems*; National Institute of Standards and Technology (NIST) *System Protection Profile for Industrial Control Systems* (SPP ICS); and NIST Federal Information Processing Standards Publication (FIPS) 199, *Standards for Security Categorization of Federal Information and Information Systems*. Three additional NIST publications that provide valuable information-assurance guidance and are useful in securing computing systems and networks are also summarized. These documents are NIST Special Publication 800-37, *Guide for the Security Certification and Accreditation of*

Federal Information Systems; NIST Special Publication 800-53, *Recommended Security Controls for Federal Information Systems*; and NIST Special Publication 800-53A, *Guide for Assessing the Security Controls in Federal Information Systems.*

ISO/IEC 17799:2005 and BS 7799-2:2002

The British Standard for Information Security Management has two parts:

1. *Code of Practice for Information Security Management*, International Organization for Standardization/International Electrotechnical Commission (ISO/IEC) 1779:2005

2. *Specification for Information Security Management Systems*, designated as BS 7799-2:2002

ISO/IEC 1779:2005 is designed to serve as a single source for best practices in the field of information security and presents a range of controls applicable to most situations. It provides high-level, voluntary guidance for information security management.

BS 7799-2:2002 presents requirements for building, maintaining, and documenting information-security management systems (ISMSs). As such, it lists recommendations for establishing an efficient information-security management framework. BS 7799-2:2002 is also used as the basis of a certification assessment of an organization.

Both documents address the following set of controls:

- Security policy
- Organization of information security
- Asset management
- Human resources security
- Physical and environmental security
- Communications and operations management
- Access control
- Information systems acquisition, development, and maintenance
- Information Security incident management
- Business continuity management
- Compliance

ISO/IEC 1779:2005

The *Code of Practice for Information Security Management* provides recommendations for individuals charged with information-system security for their organizations. The document promulgates the standard definition of information security: Preserving the confidentiality, integrity, and availability of information. Each major heading of ISO/IEC 1779:2005 is summarized as follows:

- **Security policy:** Provides a clear direction of management intent, support, and commitment to information security through a security policy document. The document should include roles and responsibilities and be distributed and used throughout the organization.

- **Organization of information security:** Provides a management structure to establish information system security throughout the organization, including allocating information security responsibilities, establishing prior contact with law enforcement and emergency responders, and implementing access controls for the computing resources and facilities.

- **Asset management:** Accounts for and protects an organization's information system assets through compiling equipment inventories, managing classified documents, and developing procedures for classifying documents.

- **Human resources security:** Protects facilities from misuse or malicious activities by conducting security awareness training, implementing appropriate personnel policies, and using nondisclosure and confidentiality agreements.

- **Physical and environmental security:** Physically protects the information processing facilities of an organization by implementing physical access controls, conditioning power lines, providing back-up power, and establishing reuse and data remanence policies. (As an example, data remanence on magnetic disks is information that remains on the disks when they are discarded or when a computer is donated to charity.)

- **Communications and operations management:** Manages and operates information processing facilities in a secure fashion, including installing protections against malicious code, protecting storage media, implementing change control procedures, and practicing separation of duties and least privilege (that is, giving individuals the minimum privileges needed to perform their assigned tasks).

- **Access control:** Controls access to an organization's information by developing appropriate policies, implementing access controls, and providing for identification and authentication.

- **Information systems acquisition, development, and maintenance:** Incorporates security into new and modified information systems through cryptography and digital signatures, configuration management, and protecting against covert channels.

- **Information-security incident management:** Establishes incident response, reporting, recovery, and associated management procedures by setting up computer incident response teams (CIRTs) and resolving incidents.

- **Business continuity management:** Focuses on making sure that the business operations of an organization continue in the event of interruptions or a major disaster, including conducting risk analyses and developing and testing a business continuity plan.

- **Compliance:** Ensures the operation of information systems does not violate legal or contractual requirements, including copyrights, export restrictions, and organizational security policies.

BS 7799-2:2002

The *Specification for Information Security Management Systems* provides control objectives and controls in coordination with the domains specified in ISO/IEC 17799:2005. In general, BS 7799-2:2002 requires the development and documentation of an information security management system (ISMS), generating required documentation, setting up a management framework, establishing document controls, and maintaining records. The sections containing detailed control descriptions in BS 7799-2:2002 correspond to the sections in ISO/IEC 17799:2005.

BS 7799:2:2002 emphasizes developing an ISMS through an iterative PLAN-DO-CHECK-ACT cycle. The activities in each cycle are summarized as follows:

- PLAN
    - Establish scope.
    - Develop a comprehensive ISMS policy.
    - Conduct risk assessment.
    - Develop a risk treatment plan.
    - Determine control objectives and controls.
    - Develop a statement of applicability describing and justifying why the specific controls were selected and others not selected.

- DO
  - Operate selected controls.
  - Detect and respond to incidents properly.
  - Conduct security awareness training.
  - Manage resources required to accomplish security tasks.
- CHECK
  - Check intrusion detection operations.
  - Check incident handling operations.
  - Conduct internal ISMS audit.
  - Conduct a management review.
- ACT
  - Implement improvements to the ISMS in response to items identified in CHECK phase.
  - Take corrective actions in response to items identified in CHECK phase.
  - Take preventive actions in response to items identified in CHECK phase.

ISA-TR99.00.01-2004, *Security Technologies for Manufacturing and Control Systems*

In March of 2004, the SP99 Standards Committee of the Instrumentation, Systems, and Automation (ISA) Society issued technical report ISA- TR99.00.01-2004 or TR1, *Security Technologies for Manufacturing and Control Systems*. TR1 and its companion document, ISA-TR99.00.02-2004, *Integrating Electronic Security into the Manufacturing and Control Systems Environment*, TR2, employ guidance from BS 7799.

In TR1, 28 electronic security technologies divided into six categories applicable to manufacturing and control systems are covered. The six categories are:

- Authentication and authorization
- Filtering/blocking/access control
- Encryption and data validation
- Audit, measurement, monitoring, and detection tools
- Computer software
- Physical security

The technologies are discussed relative to the following areas:

- Known weaknesses
- Future directions
- Assessment of use in SCADA environments
- Typical deployments
- Vulnerabilities targeted
- Recommendations and guidance
- Information sources and reference material

TR1 provides guidance for using the electronic security technologies, but does not recommend one technology over another. The technologies evaluated under the six headings are summarized as follows:

- **Authentication and authorization technologies:** Technologies include role-based authorization devices, challenge/response authentication methods, smart cards, biometrics, and password management tools.
- **Filtering/blocking/access control technologies:** Technologies include firewalls and virtual local area networks.
- **Encryption technologies and data validation:** Methods include symmetric and public key encryption, key management, digital signatures, and virtual private networks.
- **Audit, measurement, monitoring, and detection tools:** Tools include audit logs, virus detection, intrusion detection, vulnerability scanners, and automated software management.
- **Computer software:** Typical software includes operating systems and Web-related software.
- **Physical security controls:** Controls include physical protection and personnel security mechanisms.

ISA-TR99.00.02-2004, *Integrating Electronic Security into the Manufacturing and Control Systems Environment*

ISA-TR99.00.02-2004 or TR2 provides a more detailed discussion of SCADA information security methodologies and technologies than TR1. It develops these areas through a security lifecycle and discusses specific components of a security program for the manufacturing and control environment. The TR2 document also addresses auditing functions and assurance evaluation. It can be applied to a variety of control systems including distributed control systems, SCADA systems, batch and discrete process control systems, networked sensing systems, and multivariable control.

ISA-TR99.00.02-2004 follows the guidance of British Standard for Information Security Management as articulated in the following domains:

- Security policy
- Organization of information security
- Asset management
- Human resources security
- Physical and environmental security
- Communications and operations management
- Access control
- Information-systems acquisition, development, and maintenance
- Information-security incident management
- Business continuity management
- Compliance

TR2 develops a security lifecycle model comprising critical elements and provides guidance on applying each element to the manufacturing and control system at hand. These elements include assessing and defining the existing system, performing a risk analysis, implementing countermeasures, developing test plans, validating the system, and conducting periodic audits.

GAO-04-140T, *Critical Infrastructure Protection, Challenges in Securing Control Systems*

Document GAO-04-140T, *Critical Infrastructure Protection, Challenges in Securing Control Systems*, details the testimony of Robert F. Dacey, Government Accountability Office (GAO) director of information security issues, before the U.S. House Committee on Government Reform Subcommittee on Technology, Information Policy, Intergovernmental Relations, and the Census.

In his testimony on October 1, 2003, Mr. Dacey summarized the following principal factors contributing to the increased vulnerability of SCADA systems:

- Use of standard technologies with known vulnerabilities
- Connecting SCADA networks to outside networks
- Limitations of using extant security methods and techniques

- Unsecured remote connections
- Increased availability of information about SCADA systems

To counter potential new threats against control systems, Dacey proposed the following measures:

- Researching and developing new information security technologies applicable to SCADA systems
- Developing security standards, policies, and guidance for control systems
- Increasing security awareness and exchanging information among control system personnel
- Installing effective security management programs
- Developing and testing continuity plans to ensure that control systems can continue operating in the event of an outage or disaster

In addition, Dacey detailed the following six sources of potential attacks to the U.S. critical infrastructures as identified by the FBI:

- Criminal groups
- Foreign intelligence services
- Hackers
- Nations engaged in information warfare
- Insiders
- Virus writers

Dacey further outlined activities that an attacker might initiate to disrupt control systems. These activities include the following:

- Making unauthorized changes to instructions in PLCs, RTUs, and other controllers
- Delaying or blocking the flow of information through SCADA networks
- Sending false information to control system operators
- Interfering with the operation of safety systems
- Modifying control system software
- Physically breaching control system areas

Dacey also made the point that, because SCADA system computer resources are limited, applying security controls that require additional processing capacity might seriously degrade SCADA system performance.

NIST, *System Protection Profile for Industrial Control Systems* (SPP ICS)

In order to emphasize the need for SCADA security, NIST supported the establishment of the Process Control Security Requirements Forum (PCSRF) in 2001. In that year, the forum issued a draft of the *System Protection Profile for Industrial Control Systems* (SPP ICS). The PCSRF based its efforts on the Common Criteria evaluation method adopted by the international community. The SPP ICS addresses the following SCADA security issues:

- Encryption, where necessary and applicable
- Identification and authorization of users and data
- Auditing and monitoring to isolate and identify attacks
- Countermeasures to prevent spoofing attacks
- Use of product with security features enabled as the default condition
- Development and use of security policies and procedures
- Providing for physical security of the SCADA system

By using the Common Criteria system protection profile provided by the PCSRF, vendors can develop products that are available off the shelf with configurable security options tailored to SCADA systems. Appendix B provides excerpts of the SPP ICS for additional reference.

Federal Information Processing Standards Publication (FIPS Pub) 199, *Standards for Security Categorization of Federal Information and Information Systems*, February 2004

FIPS Publication 199 defines standards for categorizing information and information systems. The document specifies three categories of potential impact that a realized threat might have on an information system. In our case, the threat would be directed against a vulnerability in a SCADA system. Table 6-1 summarizes the impact levels described in FIPS Pub 199.

Based on the impact categories, FIPS 199 proposes a general formula for defining a security category (SC) of an information type. Here is the general formula:

$$\text{SC}_{\text{information type}} = \{(\textbf{confidentiality}, \textit{impact}), (\textbf{integrity}, \textit{impact}), (\textbf{availability}, \textit{impact})\}$$

Table 6-1 Potential Impact of Threat Realized

SECURITY OBJECTIVE	LOW IMPACT	MODERATE IMPACT	HIGH IMPACT
Confidentiality: Preserving authorized restrictions on information access and disclosure, including means for protecting personal privacy and proprietary information.	The unauthorized disclosure of information could be expected to have a limited adverse effect on an organization's operations, assets, or individuals.	The unauthorized disclosure of information could be expected to have a serious adverse effect on an organization's operations, assets, or individuals.	The unauthorized disclosure of information could be expected to have a severe or catastrophic adverse effect on an organization's operations, assets, or individuals.
Integrity: Guarding against improper information modification or destruction, and ensuring information nonrepudiation and authenticity.	The unauthorized modification or destruction of information could be expected to have a limited adverse effect on an organization's operations, assets, or individuals.	The unauthorized modification or destruction of information could be expected to have a serious adverse effect on an organization's operations, assets, or individuals.	The unauthorized modification or destruction of information could be expected to have a severe or catastrophic adverse effect on an organization's operations, assets, or individuals.
Availability: Ensuring timely and reliable access to and use of information.	The disruption of access to or use of information or an information system could be expected to have a limited adverse effect on an organization's operations, assets, or individuals.	The disruption of access to or use of information or an information system could be expected to have a serious adverse effect on an organization's operations, assets, or individuals.	The disruption of access to or use of information or an information system could be expected to have a severe or catastrophic adverse effect on an organization's operations, assets, or individuals.

In this formula, the acceptable values for potential impact are low, moderate, high, or not applicable.

The general formula can be applied to different types of information systems, including SCADA systems. For example, assume that a data acquisition and control system in an oil refinery is monitoring a sensor providing the temperature in a distillation tower and also reading another data stream with information on the identity of one of the plant operators. Using the definitions in Table 6-1, the loss of distillation-tower temperature sensor data would have a low potential impact regarding the security objective of confidentiality, a high potential impact with regard to integrity, and a high potential impact with regard to availability. For the operator data stream, there would be a low potential impact on confidentially, a moderate potential impact on integrity, and a low potential impact on availability.

Substituting this information in the general equation yields the following security categories for the two types of data:

$SC_{\text{distillation sensor}}$ = {(**confidentiality**, LOW), (**integrity**, HIGH), (**availability**, HIGH)}

$SC_{\text{operator information}}$ = {(**confidentiality**, LOW), (**integrity**, MODERATE), (**availability**, LOW}

FIPS 199 also states that the security category of the total system is obtained by using the highest value for each of the elements in the equation. Thus, if the SCADA system comprised only the two data inputs of our example, the security category of the SCADA system would be represented as follows:

$SC_{\text{SCADA system}}$ = {(**confidentiality**, LOW), (**integrity**, HIGH), (**availability**, HIGH)}

Additional Useful NIST Special Publications

Three additional documents published by NIST provide valuable guidance on securing computer systems and networks that is applicable to SCADA systems. These documents are summarized in the following sections.

NIST Special Publication 800-37, *Guide for the Security Certification and Accreditation of Federal Information Systems*

NIST SP 800-37 outlines tasks that government agencies must perform "to develop, document, and implement an agency-wide information security program." Even though these tasks are directed at government agencies, they are also applicable to SCADA systems if the characteristics and requirements of these systems are kept in mind. The elements covered in SP 800-37 are:

- Periodic assessments of risk
- Policies and procedures that are based on risk assessments
- Subordinate plans for providing adequate information security for networks, facilities, information systems, or groups of information systems, as appropriate
- Security awareness training
- Periodic testing and evaluation of the effectiveness of information security policies, procedures, practices, and security controls
- A process for planning, implementing, evaluating, and documenting remedial action to address any deficiencies in the information security policies, procedures, and practices
- Procedures for detecting, reporting, and responding to security incidents
- Plans and procedures to ensure continuity of operations for information systems

NIST Special Publication 800-53, *Recommended Security Controls for Federal Information Systems*

NIST SP 800-53 was issued in February 2005 in order "to provide guidelines for selecting and specifying security controls for information systems supporting the executive agencies of the federal government." The document covers 17 information-system security controls and their categorization according to Federal Information Processing Standards (FIPS) 199, *Standards for Security Categorization of Federal Information and Information Systems*. The security controls are categorized under management, operational, and technical class headings as follows:

- Management
  - Risk assessment
  - Planning
  - System and services acquisition
  - Certification, accreditation, and security assessments
- Operational
  - Personnel security
  - Physical and environmental protection

- Contingency planning
- Configuration management
- Operational maintenance
- System and information integrity
- Media protection
- Incident response
- Awareness and training
- Technical
  - Identification and authentication
  - Access control
  - Audit and accountability
  - System and communications protection

In SP 800-53, management, operational, and technical controls are defined as follows:

- **Management controls:** Safeguards or countermeasures that focus on the management of risk and the management of information system security
- **Operational controls:** Safeguards or countermeasures that primarily are implemented and executed by people (as opposed to systems)
- **Technical controls:** Safeguards or countermeasures that are primarily implemented and executed by the information system through mechanisms contained in the hardware, software, or firmware components of the system

NIST Special Publication 800-53A, *Guide for Assessing the Security Controls in Federal Information Systems*

The initial public draft of NIST SP 800-53A was issued in July 2005 "to provide guidelines for assessing the effectiveness of security controls employed in information systems supporting the executive agencies of the federal government." The assessment guidelines apply to five of the 17 security controls defined in NIST SP 800-53. Guidelines for the remainder of the controls will be included in the final version of SP 800-53A scheduled to be released by the end of 2005. The methods described in SP 800-53A are designed to enable consistent, repeatable, cost-effective security control assessments and provide a better understanding of risks to the organizational assets and information systems.

The document defines an information system as "a discrete set of information resources organized expressly for the collection, processing, maintenance, use, sharing, dissemination, or disposition of information."

NIST SP 800-53A recommends that organizations supplement the assessment procedures described in the document, especially in relation to organizational dependencies and dependencies of hardware, software, and firmware resulting from the implementation of security controls.

Summary

As a technical field develops and matures, standards, guidelines, and reference documents are generated that provide instruction on the best practices in the field. This situation is occurring in SCADA applications where custom, ad hoc practices were used early in the development of control systems. Then, as the field progressed, standard protocols and technologies were employed. Consequently, groups of control system professionals from a variety of fields, including manufacturing, the chemical industry, power generation organizations, oil refining, and water and sewage treatment, combined their knowledge to generate standards and guidelines through various professional organizations. These reference documents are continually being improved and revised. They are a valuable resource for the SCADA community in implementing security mechanisms that accommodate the special characteristics of control systems.

SCADA Security Management Implementation Issues and Guidelines

Corporate management views SCADA security from a variety of perspectives. On one hand, these officers are sincerely concerned about the safety of their country and the nation's critical infrastructure. On the other hand, when they have to make budgetary and commitment decisions for their own organization, these concerns are superceded by economic issues, tradeoffs with other critical needs, lower cost competition, catching up on deferred maintenance, and different, conflicting institutional cultures. This chapter looks at management positions concerning SCADA security priorities, SCADA culture conflicts, and other unique characteristics, and then offers some disciplined approaches for management to apply to SCADA security issues.

Management Impressions of SCADA Security

Most senior managers of companies employing SCADA systems in their major operations view security costs as a competitive economic issue. They do not see a market incentive for spending large amounts of capital on information security technology. Securing SCADA systems involves more than just purchasing and installing hardware and software. An organization has to invest in hiring appropriate personnel, training other employees, and replacing old and dated equipment. Just as some of these companies assert that regulations requiring expenditures for pollution controls negatively impact their bottom line, many claim that the costs of SCADA security will put them at a competitive disadvantage with companies that do not implement similar measures. In addition, many managers do not see investments in their individual organizations having much effect on the overall public welfare. To level the playing field, the government must develop and enforce standards for securing SCADA systems that apply to all organizations in an industry so that all the participants bear the costs equally.

The following is a list of other issues affecting the implementation of security controls in SCADA systems:

- Because of limited computing capacity, addition of security technologies might result in degrading system performance and response times.

- Use of encryption, strong authentication, configuration control, and other strong security measures usually reduce the ease of use of SCADA systems.

- Industry consolidation, increased competition, and low margins in some sectors have reduced investment in technology.

- Minimal reserve capacity, such as in the electric utility industry, has resulted in systems that are less resilient to accidents and attacks.

- Deregulation of some industries has caused them to focus on efficiency and return on investment rather on security and reliability.

- Privacy rights issues inhibit screening and profiling of some personnel.

- Many SCADA systems are older and were designed with minimal attention to security. They typically send information unencrypted and many use wireless transmission, which is susceptible to interception.

- Federal and state governments do not currently provide sufficient incentives to encourage private sector investment in SCADA security.

- Many critical infrastructure systems have a history of deferred maintenance that has to be addressed before implementing a security system.

SCADA Culture

SCADA and distributed control systems have traditionally been the domain of electrical engineers. With the transition to standard hardware and software platforms, Internet protocols, and connections to corporate enterprise networks, IT personnel are becoming more involved with SCADA systems. Thus, there are conflicting cultures and priorities and differing stances on implementing intrusion detection systems, firewalls, authentication, and encryption.

Fortunately for us, the view that because of their very nature most SCADA systems are less vulnerable than IT systems to cyberattacks is fading. It is true that control systems *were* less visible than IT systems and many were not connected to external networks. Also, their components required detailed technological knowledge to implement and operate. Thus, there the myth of security-through-obscurity had some basis in fact.

Information on SCADA systems and potential security problems started to become publicly available because of the Y2K situation. Additional awareness, often worrisome, came with information associated with the President's Commission on Critical Infrastructure Protection. Such information was and remains available on Web sites and through popular literature. Engineering and other technical societies make knowledge of SCADA systems and their components available through educational efforts and seminars. Manufacturers of SCADA elements provide detailed product information in brochures and Web sites. Newspaper and Web articles now continually list threats and vulnerabilities to U.S. nuclear plants, utilities, refineries, rail systems, ports, water systems, and other portions of the nation's critical infrastructure.

Unique Characteristics and Requirements of SCADA Systems

Most network and computer security controls have been developed for IT systems, which, as discussed throughout this text, do not have the same operating and maintenance characteristics as SCADA systems. SCADA systems have to be available all day, every day, cannot be shut down for running back-ups, have to have deterministic response times, should not accidentally lock out operators in crisis situations, do not usually have excess computing capacity, and might have life and death consequences if malfunctions occur.

For example, if a SCADA implementation uses Internet protocols and Web servers to poll RTUs for data, an interruption in the communication from the Web server might cause the polling to restart. Because the server is handling many clients, the polling might take a long time to complete because of restarts. A better approach is a *push* architecture, wherein the RTU sends data to the master station at specific time intervals or when other conditions are met.

The user interface is another area where SCADA and IT requirements differ. Too much information, such as graphics, schematics, and large amounts of raw data on SCADA screens, can tend to overwhelm the operator and make it difficult to detect critical situations in a timely fashion.

Limitations of Current Technologies

Because of the unique nature of SCADA applications relative to IT systems, additional research and development are needed for security technologies tailored to SCADA systems. An example of one such effort is the National SCADA Testbed developed by the Center for SCADA Security, a program of the Sandia National Laboratories. The Testbed is sponsored by the DOE Office of Energy Assurance and is a joint effort with the Idaho National Engineering and Environmental Laboratory (INEEL). The Testbed conducts SCADA security research and development in the following areas:

- Cryptographic security
- Autonomous agents
- System assessment
- Communication and control
- Generation and load facilities for distributed energy resources
- Secure protocols
- System vulnerability analysis
- Secure architecture design
- Self-healing technology
- Intrusion detection

Another joint effort between the Sandia National Laboratories and the Los Alamos National Laboratory is the National Infrastructure Simulation and Analysis Center. This center is focusing on modeling and simulation to better understand and improve the security of the nation's critical infrastructures. Some additional SCADA security research, development, and standards efforts are given in Table 7-1.

Table 7-1 Some SCADA R&D and Standards Efforts

ORGANIZATION	ACTIVITY
National Institute of Standards and Technology (NIST)	Process Controls Security Requirements Forum (PCSRF) for developing specifications and certification processes
Instrumentation, Systems, and Automation Society (ISA)	Standards for the security of manufacturing and control systems
Electric Power Institute (EPRI)	Guidelines for interoperability for real-time data interchange among utilities (utility communications architecture)

Table 7-1   *(continued)*

ORGANIZATION	ACTIVITY
Gas Technology Institute	Encryption algorithms for control systems
Chemical Sector Cybersecurity Program	Common security vulnerability assessment methodology
British Columbia Institute of Technology	Tracks industrial control security incidents and conducts tests on control system architectures and products

Guidance for Management in SCADA Security Investment

Systems engineering provides a basis for designing secure SCADA systems, but this approach requires an investment in time, personnel, and funds. The DoD has adopted a systems engineering approach to information-system security that management can promote for application to SCADA systems.

The Information Assurance Technical Framework Forum (IATFF) has developed the IATF document, Release 3.1, which provides guidance for the protection of information systems. The purpose of the IATFF is to encourage technical interchanges on the topic of information assurance among academia, government, and industry.

Information-System Security Engineering

IATF 3.1 defines the following information-system security engineering (ISSE) processes:

- Discover information protection needs
- Define system security requirements
- Design system security architecture
- Develop detailed security design
- Implement system security

These processes provide valuable insight applicable to securing SCADA systems.

Discover Information Protection Needs

This process of discovering information protection needs is designed to provide an understanding of the performance requirements of the SCADA system components and ensure that the implementation will meet those requirements. This activity begins with gathering all available information concerning the project and its mission. In gathering and processing the information, the following items should be kept in mind:

- Agreements or contracts
- Information generators
- Information users
- Processes being used
- User roles

The acquired information can be used to determine potential threats to the SCADA system, impacts of threats realized, and corresponding potential security controls. In this process, items such as personnel roles and responsibilities, priorities, and design constraints have to be considered.

Define System Security Requirements

The desired outcome of the effort to define system security requirements is a solution set that meets the SCADA security requirements developed out of the process of discovering information protection needs. To determine the correct solution set, the security engineer has to identify the SCADA system boundaries that have to be protected, generate unambiguous system requirements, analyze the flow of data, and identify services provided by other elements. These activities and results should be documented in detail.

Design System Security Architecture

The process of designing system security architecture includes identifying the functional requirements generated in the previous step and selecting the appropriate controls and services to implement them. Examples of these controls and services are:

- Digital signatures
- Encryption
- Key management

Develop Detailed Security Design

The elements of detailed security design development include the following activities:

- Placing the design documents under configuration control.
- Cataloging candidate off-the-shelf (COTS) products.
- Cataloging custom security products.
- Developing specifications such as Common Criteria protection profiles.
- Ensuring that the components in the design address both technical and nontechnical information security mechanisms.
- Evaluating tradeoffs among cost, priorities, performance, schedule, and remaining security risks.

Implement System Security

Implementing system security takes the SCADA security system to the operational phase. In this phase, component availability, cost, form factor, reliability, and ability to meet specifications have to be considered. In order to ensure that the security controls that have been put in place are performing properly, a systems effectiveness assessment has to be performed. This assessment evaluates the following items:

- The ability of the security controls to protect against the identified threats
- System life-cycle support plans
- Compatibility with operational procedures
- Maintenance training materials
- Evaluation criteria compliance

Also, this process includes performing the following tasks:

- Developing test procedures
- Planning for tests to ensure that appropriate personnel facilities and other necessary resources are available
- Conducting component testing
- Conducting integration testing
- Conducting functional testing

- Conducting interface and graphical user interface testing

- Generating test reports

- Documenting other required procedures, such as installation, operation, and maintenance

- Conducting training on all critical processes and procedures

Common Criteria Protection Profiles

In Chapter 6 of this text, the NIST/PCSRF *System Protection Profile for Industrial Control Systems* (SPP ICS) is reviewed. This document, excerpted in Appendix B, uses the Common Criteria Protection Profile to define SCADA security issues so that vendors can develop products using these evaluation criteria. These protection profiles are implementation-independent and comprise the following elements:

- Assumptions

- Rationale

- Security-related functional requirements

- Security objectives

- Information assurance requirements

The IATF Web site at www.iatf.net/protection_profiles/ provides additional protection profiles for switches, routers, mobile code, firewalls, and biometrics.

Defense-in-Depth

Another security approach used by federal and defense organizations is the principle of defense-in-depth. Defense-in-depth is built on the three critical elements of people, technology, and operations and comprises the following steps:

- Defending the network and infrastructure

- Defending the enclave boundary

- Defending the computing environment

- Defending the supporting infrastructures

The enclave referred to in the list is defined by DoD Directive 8500.1, *Information Assurance (IA)*, October 24, 2002, as a "collection of computing environments connected by one or more internal networks under the control of a single authority and security policy, including personnel and physical security." Examples of enclaves include local area networks, data processing centers, and backbone networks.

People

SCADA system management personnel have to be committed to a SCADA security program. This commitment is manifest in the actions depicted in Figure 7-1.

Technology

In order to achieve the required protections for SCADA systems, an organization has to develop policies for the acquisition of appropriate technology. Figure 7-2 summarizes the elements necessary for a good technology acquisition program.

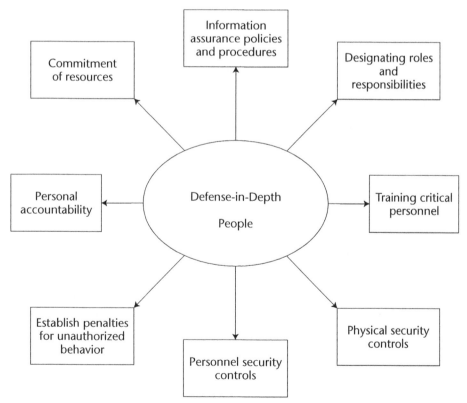

Figure 7-1   SCADA management commitment

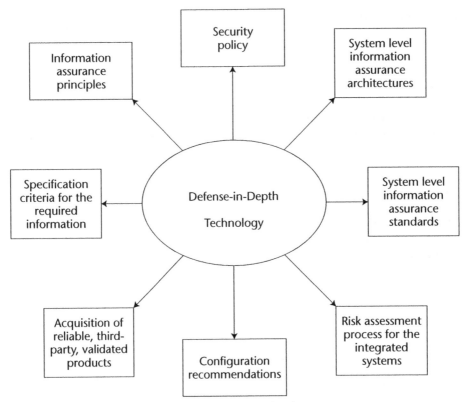

Figure 7-2   Technology acquisition in defense-in-depth

Operations

During the day-to-day operations of a SCADA system, it is important to ensure that the security controls are in place and functioning properly. Figure 7-3 lists the important relevant information security–related operations activities.

Defense-in-Depth Strategy

The defense-in-depth strategy promotes defense in multiple places and locations, layering defenses, robustness of information security components, the application of intrusion detection systems, and deployment of robust public key management methods.

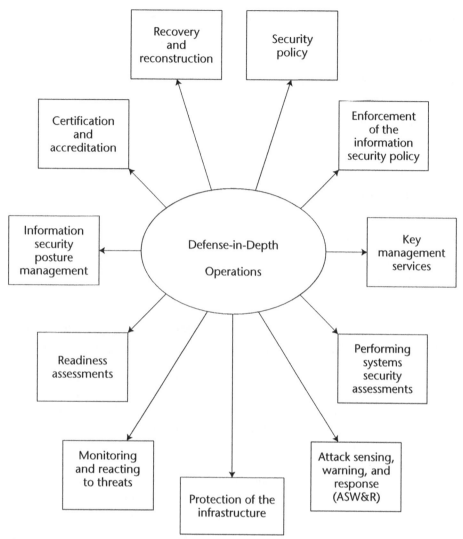

Figure 7-3 Operations security controls

IATF 3.1 provides the following guidelines for accomplishing defense-in-depth:

■ Employ available commercial off-the-shelf (COTS) products and use in-house development for those items not otherwise available.

■ Conduct vulnerability assessments.

■ Conduct security and security awareness training.

- Plan for malicious and accidental harmful events.

- Overlap security controls so that the failure or circumvention of a single control does not compromise the overall information infrastructure.

- Ensure that only cleared and authorized personnel have physical access to the facilities.

- Set up intrusion detection and reporting plans.

IATF 3.1 also defines the following types of attacks to defend against:

- **Passive:** Interception of passwords, monitoring open communications

- **Active:** Viruses, stealing information, breaking encryption

- **Close in:** Attacks by attaining physical proximity to networks

- **Insider:** Malicious or accidental attacks by insiders

- **Distribution:** Malicious modification of software at the factory or during distribution of the software

The NIST SP 800-14, *Generally Accepted Principles and Practices for Securing Information Technology Systems*

Another useful document that provides management guidance applicable to securing SCADA Systems is NIST Special Publication 800-14, published in September 1996. This document builds on the Organization for Economic Cooperation and Development (OECD) guidelines (www.oecd.org) for cybersecurity. SP 800-14 defines eight information-system security principles and 14 common security practices, which have relevance to securing control systems. Again, the special requirements of SCADA systems have to be kept in mind, but these principles and practices are an excellent roadmap for management to SCADA system security. Here are the eight SP 800-14 principles:

- Computer security supports the mission of the organization.

- Computer security is an integral element of sound management.

- Computer security should be cost-effective.

- Systems owners have security responsibilities outside their own organizations.

- Computer security responsibilities and accountability should be made explicit.

- Computer security requires a comprehensive and integrated approach.

- Computer security should be periodically reassessed.

- Computer security is constrained by societal factors.

The 14 computer security practices recommended by SP 800-14 are listed as follows:

- An organization should have a computer security program policy, a policy to focus on specific issues, and a system specific policy to address management decisions.

- There should be centralized management and oversight of computer security at multiple levels in the organization.

- A risk management program for assessing risk, taking steps to reduce risk to an acceptable level, and maintaining that level of risk should be put in place.

- Computer security should be planned and managed throughout the system life cycle. The system life cycle comprises

  - Initiation

  - Development/acquisition

  - Implementation

  - Operation/maintenance

  - Disposal

- Personnel issues that involve users, managers, and implementers along with their appropriate access authorizations have to be addressed.

- Plan to ensure that the system will continue operating in the event of a disaster or interruption.

- Implement incident handling procedures to respond rapidly and effectively to malicious code and intrusions.

- Conduct security awareness training for all appropriate personnel.

- Ensure that external support functions and systems administrators practice information-system security principles.

- Implement physical and environmental security controls.

- Require identification and authentication to obtain access privileges to system resources.

- Implement technical (logical) access control mechanisms.

- Provide for audit trails of system activity to detect intrusions, establish accountability, analyze past events, and find problems.

- Apply cryptography and digital signatures where applicable and relevant.

NIST Special Publication 800-26, *Security Self-Assessment Guide for Information Technology Systems*

A valuable tool that managers responsible for SCADA systems can use to detect vulnerabilities and improve the security of these systems is the self-assessment. NIST SP 800-26, *Security Self-Assessment Guide for Information Technology Systems,* November 2001, provides a questionnaire approach that leads an organization through an effective computer-security self-assessment process. Even though the publication refers to IT systems, the information security elements that are covered have direct application to SCADA system security. Again, the deterministic, availability, real-time, and round-the-clock requirements of SCADA systems must be kept in mind when applying the self-assessment questionnaire.

The self-assessment process begins by "defining boundaries around a set of processes, communications, storage, and related resources. The elements within these boundaries constitute a single system requiring a system security plan and a security evaluation whenever a major modification to the system occurs." Components of systems within a boundary must have the same operational objectives and security requirements and be under the same direct management control.

The topic areas covered by the self-assessment questionnaire in SP 800-26 are:

- Management controls
  - Risk management
  - Review of security controls
  - Life-cycle maintenance
  - Authorize processing (certification and accreditation)
  - System security plan
- Operational controls
  - Personnel security
  - Physical security
  - Production, input/output controls
  - Contingency planning
  - Hardware and systems software
  - Data integrity
  - Documentation

- Security awareness, training, and education
- Incident response capability
- Technical controls
  - Identification and authentication
  - Logical access controls
  - Audit trails

SP 800-26 defines five levels of effectiveness for each answer in the security assessment questionnaire. These levels are listed here:

- **Level 1:** Control objective is documented in a security policy.
- **Level 2:** Security controls are documented as procedures.
- **Level 3:** Procedures have been implemented.
- **Level 4:** Procedures and security controls are tested and reviewed.
- **Level 5:** Procedures and security controls are fully integrated into a comprehensive program.

Summary

In spite of the increased awareness of the vulnerability of SCADA systems to accidental or malicious incidents, many organizations have yet to take action to implement SCADA security controls. Conversely, some companies have instituted a few SCADA security mechanisms and are overly optimistic about the invulnerability of their systems. Yet others rationalize that the threat to SCADA applications is minimal because such systems are not as visible or well understood as IT systems.

This chapter covers the different cultures and conflicts related to SCADA systems. As illustrated in Figure 7-4, SCADA implementations now might involve integration into corporate enterprise networks, come under the jurisdiction of IT departments, have to justify security against other corporate expenditures, and deal with lower cost installations by competitors. However, through a disciplined program of instituting policies and procedures, management commitment, application of best practices, research and development aimed at SCADA security solutions, government incentives, and training, sound SCADA programs can be successfully planned and put into operation. The resulting systems will provide the required security at reasonable expense and make the nation's infrastructures robust and defensible.

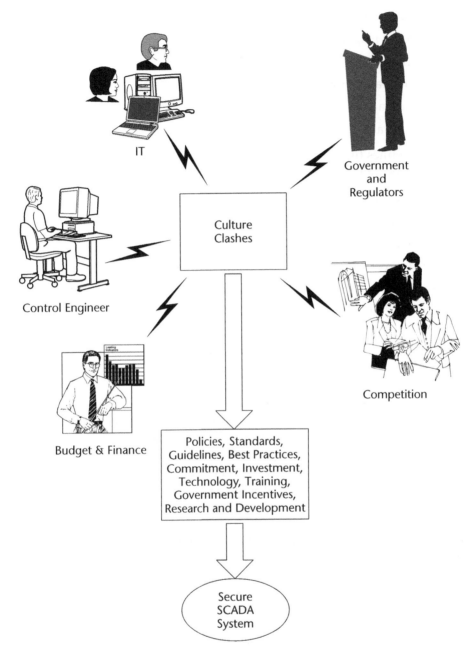

Figure 7-4 SCADA security programs in the enterprise

Where We Stand Today

With the increasing awareness of SCADA system threats and potential avenues of attack on these systems, it is reasonable to ask, "How vulnerable are we?" In order to answer this question with some measure of specificity, this chapter summarizes today's state of affairs and explores the status of three important sectors of the U.S. critical infrastructure in which SCADA systems are a fundamental component. These sectors are the oil and gas industry, rail systems, and maritime systems.

The Status Today

With the increasing linkage between process control and IT departments in many organizations, the responsibility for process control security is being assigned to the IT departments by default. IT departments are usually not familiar with process control equipment, up-time requirements, and reliability concerns associated with SCADA systems. Thus, there are gaps in the protection of SCADA systems that can be exploited by internal and external threats. Of primary concern is the accessibility of the SCADA network from remote nodes and Internet connections. Because they share an enterprise LAN, corporate IT traffic such as e-mail and VoIP traffic might be intermingled with EtherNet/IP or MODBUS/TCP protocols from the SCADA system.

A typical and sometimes-necessary situation in a control environment is the sharing of passwords. In the event of an emergency, it could be calamitous if someone could not terminate a dangerous event because he or she did not know or forgot the passwords to the myriad of control elements in a large chemical or nuclear facility. Another aspect of passwords is that in most SCADA environments, they are sent in plain text over networks and are not encrypted as mandated by good security practices.

A different concern regarding the security of critical infrastructure elements is their ease of access by the public. Reservoirs, dams, water treatment facilities, pipelines, and even some electrical and chemical plants can be accessed without intervention. Many SCADA system components that are a part of these structures also are not very well protected and might be physically accessible.

Another critical issue is that many critical infrastructure components, water systems for example, have been victims of deferred maintenance and are in poor physical condition. Restoring these facilities to a robust and up-to-date status will go a long way toward increasing their resistance to malicious attacks and accidents.

Because the life cycle of control systems might span 10 to 20 years or more, many of these systems are old, relative to IT equipment. Thus, they are vulnerable to attacks and do not have the capacity to support security controls such as antivirus software. Many of these controls have programs burned into read-only memory (ROM) that cannot be changed easily. Other components might be physically difficult to access or replace without causing damage to the equipment. An additional complication is that the manufacturer of the equipment might have gone out of business.

A common recommendation for protecting networks, including SCADA networks, is to employ a firewall. However, firewalls that can filter application-layer SCADA packets employing protocols such as EtherNet/IP or MODBUS/TCP are rare. Also, SCADA messaging is usually assigned to a single port such as port 502/tcp and is, therefore, amenable to probing and intrusion by a malicious attacker.

These issues are summarized in Figure 8-1.

Human Issues

An insider poses one of the most serious threats to the security of SCADA systems. An individual who is employed by an organization, who has access to the SCADA system components, and who might have technical knowledge can cause serious damage to equipment and loss of life if he or she decides to sabotage critical control elements. Vetting of employees and outside contractors that have access to control system components can go a long way toward reducing the risk to our critical infrastructures.

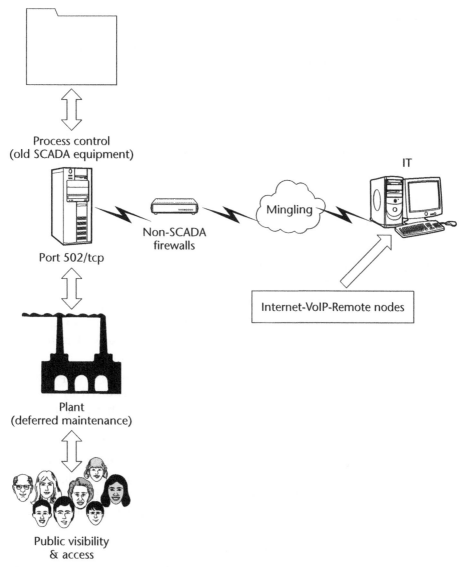

Figure 8-1 SCADA security issues

A related issue is that consequences of attacks are usually multiplied if they occur during other disrupting events or problems in operations. A plant shutdown or startup makes it more vulnerable to malfunctions, even without external intrusions by attackers. A successful malicious act during these periods would increase the probability of larger damage and destruction. A counter, but not a cure to this situation, is employee training, emergency planning, and backup strategies.

Weakness of Standard Security Approaches

Conventional cybersecurity approaches generally focus on standalone products that are associated with individual devices on a network. This point-oriented security approach is vulnerable to attacks that circumvent the one particular security control. In addition, other parts of the network might be unaware that an attack is occurring. What is needed is a coordinated security paradigm that takes advantage of the capabilities of devices such as routers and switches that are cognizant of network activities on a larger scale. Research efforts are underway in many organizations to develop adaptive network and application-aware solutions that address security as a collaboration of defense mechanisms operating as a defense system to identify threats and respond accordingly.

The Oil and Gas Industry

SCADA systems are used extensively in the oil and gas industry, which provides the U.S. with approximately two-thirds of its energy. SCADA applications include monitoring pipeline flows, controlling processes at refineries, and regulating oil pumping and natural gas compressor stations.

The oil and gas sector comprises approximately 200,000 miles of oil pipelines and two million miles of gas pipelines. Crude oil is transported by smaller pipelines from domestic wells to larger trunk lines, which transport both domestic and imported crude oil to regional locations. At these points, the oil is refined into gasoline and other types of petroleum products. Then, the refined products are carried by another network of pipelines to distribution centers, from which trucks carry these products to service stations. In the United States, 146 refineries incorporate SCADA systems in one form or another. There are more natural gas pipelines because they also include local distribution segments that provide gas to the consumer.

The sheer number of pipelines, refineries, and distribution centers, most of which involve SCADA systems, makes it obvious that SCADA security in this sector is a major concern. From the discussions in this text, it is clear that vulnerabilities do exist in these systems and these vulnerabilities have a high potential of being exploited by resolute attackers. In order to address some of these concerns, the oil and gas sector has developed the following two standards:

- The American Petroleum Institute (API) Standard 1164, *Pipeline SCADA Security*, First Edition, September 2004. (The API is made up of over 400 oil and gas industry members.)

■ The American Gas Association (AGA) *Cryptographic Protection of SCADA Communications General Recommendations,* Draft 3, AGA Report Number 12, August 14, 2004. (The AGA represents 192 natural gas utilities.)

API 1164 targets pipeline security whereas AGA 12 focuses on encryption for authentication of information exchange on SCADA networks.

API Standard 1164

Standard 1164 is intended for small-to-medium pipeline systems and provides examples of industry best practices and practices to "harden the core architecture." It also identifies processes for determining and analyzing pipeline SCADA system vulnerabilities. The main topics in API 1164 are listed here:

■ Communication

■ Access control

■ Physical security

■ Information distribution

■ Management system

■ Network design and data interchange

Appendix A in Standard 1164 contains a checklist guide for evaluating SCADA system security, and Appendix B illustrates an example of a security plan for a SCADA control system. The Appendix A checklist addresses the following areas:

■ Authentication

■ Change and problem management

■ Network connectivity

■ Application and database

■ Personnel security

■ System security audit and review

■ Physical security

■ Computer, telephone, and network usage

■ Information retention/archive/backup

■ Information classification and application criticality

■ Contractors, vendors, consultants, and third parties

The security plan in Appendix B comprises sections on identification, documentation, risk analysis, preventive action, oversight, and security management.

AGA Report Number 12

The AGA Report Number 12 is designed to protect SCADA systems from attacks. Protections include security policies and test plans. AGA 12, Draft 3, provides background on SCADA systems and the fundamentals of cryptography. It then covers types of attacks against SCADA systems and applying cryptography to those systems. Two annexes in AGA 12, Annex F and Annex H, provide the following guidance:

- Annex F: Security Practice Fundamentals
  - Awareness of security assurance
  - Recommendations for staffing an information security team
  - Recommendations for writing security policies
  - Auditing
  - Recommendations for performing assessment and analysis
- Annex H: Cryptographic System Test Plan
  - Test requirements and evaluation criteria
  - Special test setup requirements
  - Interoperability testing
  - Test architecture and environment
  - Test reports

Future addendums to AGA 12 will address the following cryptographic areas:

- "Retrofit Link Encryption for Asynchronous Serial Communications of SCADA Systems" (AGA 12-1)
- "Protection of IP-Based, Networked SCADA Systems" (AGA 12-2)
- "Protection Embedded in SCADA Components" (AGA 12-3)

Interdependencies

A characteristic of most SCADA systems is the interdependency among different industry sectors and within an industry sector. The oil and gas arena is no different. There are interdependencies in plants and refineries wherein a disruption in one system will propagate to other entities. For example, a SCADA attack on a pipeline or port providing feedstock to a refinery will curtail gasoline production at that refinery. The reduction in gasoline production will affect other sectors of the economy that need gasoline to function. Similarly, attacks on electric utility SCADA systems will ripple down to the other industry sectors requiring electrical power to operate. These sectors include water suppliers, transportation, chemical plants, ports, and refineries as examples. The negative economic consequences of this cascading effect can be enormous.

Important issues to consider in the interdependency scenarios are the mitigating effects of redundancy in SCADA systems, the probability of life threatening situations, amount of damage to property, time to recover, and geographic range of consequential physical and economic harm.

Rail System Security

SCADA systems are critical links in rail passenger and freight transportation systems. As with other SCADA applications, rail control systems are vulnerable to malicious attacks and human error. In order to address these and other security issues, the railroads established the Rail Industry Security Committee to facilitate coordination among the member organizations in security-related matters. In the public sector, the U.S. Department of Transportation, Federal Transit Administration (FTA), Office of Safety and Security, has initiated efforts to identify gaps in rail security, promote coordination with emergency responders, conduct security assessments, share intelligence, and educate employees.

Rail systems carrying hazardous and toxic cargos are of particular concern due to the destruction that can occur if these dangerous materials are released. In response to this threat, the freight rail industry conducted a strategic review of issues surrounding the transportation of hazardous materials. The review identified the need to improve the security of SCADA systems and the information infrastructure, to monitor control systems for signal tampering, to install video monitoring equipment, and improve personnel training.

Vulnerabilities can exist in the rail SCADA signaling and control elements. These elements and their functions are summarized in Table 8-1.

Table 8-1 Rail Signaling and Control Elements and Potential Attacks

ELEMENT	FUNCTION
Central traffic control systems	Control central operations, cab signaling, tracks.
Train to wayside communications systems	Performs master-timing, train identification, and automatic train control.
Control systems for the wayside	Monitor switch settings, communicate with other wayside devices, detect trains, and perform signaling.

(continued)

Table 8-1   *(continued)*

ELEMENT	FUNCTION
Railway crossing detection systems	Using radar, ultrasonic, magnetic or other sensors, determine if train is approaching or if there is a vehicle in the intersection.

Noting from the table that most of the signaling and control elements involve wireless communications, including sensor transmissions, attacks that jam, modify, or spoof signals could cause serious disruptions and damage to rail systems.

Some of the newer SCADA controls for rail systems are incorporating checks that attempt to avoid such attacks. For example, these systems provide rail system supervisory personnel with the ability to monitor the location of all trains as well as the signals, crossing gates, fire alarms, and intrusion alarms. Also, information from passenger stations and relay houses and other events occurring on the system are monitored and stored in a database for analysis. The SCADA system works with vital logic devices to detect conflicting and possible dangerous situations such as a train approaching a switch that has been moved to an improper position.

Here are just some examples of freight rail accidents or disruptions, some involving hazardous materials, that give some indication of the potential harm that can result from deliberate terrorist attacks:

- Toxic spill of anhydrous ammonia caused by a Canadian Pacific train derailment in North Dakota in January of 2002
- Release of chlorine in Columbia, South Carolina, in January of 2005 as a result of freight train crash caused by an incorrect switch setting
- Hydrogen fluoride spill in January of 2005 by a Norfolk Southern freight train derailment in East Deer Township, Pennsylvania
- Disruption of freight and commuter rail transportation involving Maryland, Virginia, and Washington, D.C., in August of 2003 as a result of a Sobig virus infection of signaling and dispatching systems.

Port Security

The primary focus of seaport security is on the detection of chemical, biological, and nuclear weapons, of drugs, and of illegal entry. Another area of concern that does not receive as much notoriety as the previous issues is seaport

SCADA security. The utilities that supply seaports rely on SCADA systems for their operation. In addition, these utilities are interdependent, in that a disruption in one might critically affect another. For example, if the electric power is disrupted, water pumps would cease working, and all equipment requiring electricity, such as motorized gates, spotlights, computer systems, and detection systems, would be inoperable. In the United States, dealing with such issues that affect port operations is the responsibility of local port authorities and not the U.S. government.

Seaports are usually the terminuses of a number of transportation systems. In the event of an attack on a seaport, these systems can also be disabled and have a ripple affect on the economy and security. These transportation interdependencies are illustrated in Figure 8-2.

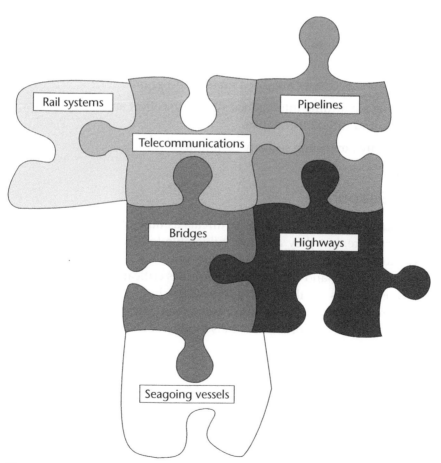

Figure 8-2   Seaport transportation interdependencies

There are 360 harbors in the United States, and an attack on one these ports would cause most of the others to close as a preventive measure. This closure would have a drastic impact on the U.S. economy because most of the material entering the country comes through seaports. Losses would be in the range of billions of dollars per day.

Legislation

The Maritime Transportation Security Act of 2002 (MTSA 2002) was signed into law by President Bush in November of 2002. This act is aimed at strengthening port security measures and includes the following stipulations:

- Instituting background checks for any persons entering secure areas at port facilities and ships
- Establishing port security plans
- Conducting vulnerability assessments of U.S. ports by the U.S. Coast Guard
- Instituting a U.S. Coast Guard sea marshal program
- Developing a maritime intelligence system to collect and analyze crew, passenger, and cargo information
- Setting up area maritime security committees

Threats to Seaports

Seaports are subject to some of the same threats as other portions of the U.S. critical infrastructure, but they also are vulnerable to some unique exploits. SCADA systems are involved in controlling electrical energy, natural gas energy, pipelines, water, and various other supplies critical to the operation of a seaport. Thus, attacks on these SCADA systems have the potential to not only shut down a port, but also to inflict damage on personnel and facilities. Other critical entities in seaports that are also vulnerable to attacks follow:

- Terminals
- Navigational systems
- Pilot boats
- Fuel depots
- Communications networks
- Computer facilities

- Security facilities
- Docks
- Cranes
- Locks

The typical sources of attacks on seaport facilities follow:

- Disgruntled employees
- Terrorists
- Thieves
- Criminals
- Smugglers
- Stowaways
- Illegal immigrants
- Spies

Countermeasures

Countermeasures that can be applied to enhance port security can be divided into two categories, conventional and advanced. Conventional countermeasures are those mechanisms that are generally applied to most information systems, while advanced measures are geared toward the special problems of seaport protection.

Conventional Countermeasures

These conventional countermeasures are familiar approaches:

- Developing and implementing security policies
- Conducting security awareness training
- Screening service and contractor personnel
- Implementing authentication mechanisms
- Using biometrics for identification and authentication
- Employing access controls
- Placing SCADA systems central controls in secure areas
- Establishing computer incident response teams (CIRTs)

- Using guards
- Installing and improving lighting
- Securing parking areas
- Establishing restricted areas
- Developing disaster recovery and business continuity plans
- Implementing SCADA system firewalls
- Employing virus scanning for SCADA systems
- Establishing authentication mechanisms

On a global scale, the United States has implemented a layered maritime security strategy that addresses security overseas at international ports, in-transit, and on U.S. shores. Examples of elements in this initiative are listed here:

- 24-hr advance manifest container security initiative
- Automated targeting system 96-hour advance notice of arrival
- Security boardings on U.S. shores
- Automatic identification system
- Radiation, chemical, bioterrorism screening
- Intelligence fusion centers
- Port security assessment program
- Nonintrusive inspection (NII) technology
- Maritime safety and security teams
- Transportation workers identity card

Advanced Countermeasures

A number of advanced technologies and research efforts are being employed to protect the U.S. seaports. The following list is a summary of the main approaches:

- The Idaho National Engineering and Environmental Laboratory SCADA Testbed is tasked with performing experiments to advance the state of SCADA system security. The Testbed is supported by the Department of Homeland Security (DHS) and the U.S. Department of Energy (DoE).

- Satellite-based communications and monitoring systems provide automatic ship identification capabilities.

- DHS Advanced Research Projects Agency (HSARPA) provides research in secure SCADA systems, tracking methods for small vessels, computer modeling of infrastructure vulnerabilities, and new chemical and biosensors.

- Radio Frequency Identification (RFID) and Global Positioning Systems (GPS) track vehicles arriving at ports and locate specific containers stored in port yards.

- Sensor fusion

- Digital imaging

Security Controls That Can Be Put in Place Now

There are specific actions that can be taken to improve the information-system security aspects of SCADA systems without waiting for the development of new technologies. These controls are generally well understood and can have a significant impact on increasing the security of seaport-related SCADA systems. These control actions are listed here:

- Employ access control for elements of SCADA systems.

- Employ SSL and IPSec, where applicable and feasible.

- Apply SCADA-aware firewalls to SCADA supervisory control elements.

- Authenticate SCADA system data to ensure it has not been modified.

- Employ and manage digital certificates and cryptographic keys used for encryption and digital signatures relating to SCADA system elements.

- Institute perimeter monitoring of remote, unattended SCADA system elements.

- Use tamper-resistant or tamper-proof enclosures for SCADA system components.

- Apply biometrics and smart card identification and authentication technologies to SCADA systems.

As with the implementation of security mechanisms to any domain, there are costs to implement these measures in seaport SCADA systems. These costs include financial, performance, space, and additional security components.

Summary

The state of SCADA system security is in flux. The good news is that the slope toward improvement is positive, even though the base starting point has a number of negatives. As the visibility and consciousness of SCADA system security is raised, the government and industry sectors are making strides to protect the SCADA components of the U.S. critical infrastructure. Government agencies and national laboratories are allocating funding to SCADA research and development and fostering cooperation among academia and the public and private sectors. Industry groups are developing standards and guidelines for helping companies protect their SCADA systems from cyber attacks.

Conversely, it is economically difficult, even unfeasible, for many organizations that are part of the critical infrastructure to undertake large-scale SCADA system security improvements on their own. Also, because many SCADA system hardware and software suppliers believe that organizations using SCADA systems do not want to invest in security upgrades, these vendors are not developing and promoting SCADA security solutions. This situation is reinforced because there have been no significant reported attacks on SCADA systems in the U.S. critical infrastructure to date.

A major concern is that the timeline for achieving SCADA security for the large number of potential targets in the U.S. is relatively long whereas vulnerabilities exist today that can be exploited. In the interim, the fruits of government, academic, and private cooperation must be conscientiously applied until the goals for protecting the infrastructure are reached.

Acronyms and Abbreviations

ACL: access control list

AES: advanced encryption standard

AGC: automatic generation control

AM/FM: automated mapping/facilities mapping

ATM: asynchronous transfer mode

BCIT: British Columbia Institute of Technology

CDPD: cellular digital packet data

CERT: computer emergency response team

CGI: common gateway interface

CHAP: challenge handshake authentication protocol

CI: critical infrastructures

CIP: Common Industrial Protocol (formerly Control and Information Protocol)

CIS: customer information systems

CPU: central processing unit

DAC: discretionary access control

DCS: distributed control system

DDE: dynamic data exchange

DDoS: distributed denial-of-service

DES: data encryption standard

DMS: distribution management systems

DMZ: demilitarized zone

DoS: denial-of-service

DSA: digital signature algorithm

EMS: energy management system

FERC: Federal Energy Regulatory Commission

FIPS: Federal Information Processing Standards

FTP: file transfer protocol

GIS: geographic information systems

GPS: global positioning system

GSM: global system for mobile

GUI: graphical user interface

HIDS: host intrusion detection system

HMI: human machine interface

HTTP: HyperText Transfer Protocol

HTTPS: HyperText Transfer Protocol Secure

I&W: indications and warnings

ICMP: Internet control message protocol

IDS: intrusion detection system

IED: intelligent electronic devices

IEEE: Institute of Electrical and Electronics Engineers

IETF: Internet engineering task force

IP: Internet protocol

IPS: intrusion prevention system

IPSEC: Internet protocol security protocol

ISA: The Instrumentation, Systems, and Automation Society

ISO: independent system operator

IS: information system

IT: information technology

LAN: local area network

MAC: media access control

MTU: master terminal unit

MSSP: managed security service provider

NAT: network address translation

NERC: North American Electric Reliability Council

NIC: network interface card

NIDS: network intrusion detection system

NIST: National Institute of Standards and Technology

NSA: National Security Agency

OEM: original equipment manufacturer

OLE: object linking and embedding

OS: operating system

PAP: password authentication protocol

PC: personal computers

PCN: process control network

PDA: personal digital assistant

PGP: pretty good privacy

PIN: personal identification number

PKI: public key infrastructure

PLC: programmable logic controller

PPP: point-to-point protocol

PSSA: power system security analysis

PX: power exchange

RBAC: role-based access control

RFC: request for comment

ROM: read-only memory

RTOS: real-time operating system

RTU: remote terminal unit

SAS: substation automation systems

SCADA: supervisory control and data acquisition

SMTP: simple mail transfer protocol

SSH: secure shell

SSL: secure socket layer

SSO: single sign on

TCP: transmission control protocol

TLS: transport layer security

TOE: target of evaluation

UCA: utility communications architecture

UDP: user datagram protocol

USB: universal serial bus

VDS: virus detection system

VLAN: virtual local area network

VPN: virtual private network

WAN: wide area network

WLAN: wireless local area network

System Protection Profile – Industrial Control Systems

Version 1.0
Prepared for NIST (National Institute of Standards and Technology) by Decisive Analytics*

Document Control

Preparation

ACTION	NAME	DATE
Prepared by:	Ron Melton, Terry Fletcher, Matt Earley	14 April 2004
Reviewed by:	Murray Donaldson	14 April 2004

*www.isd.mel.nist.gov/projects/processcontrol/PCSREF_info.pdf

Release

VERSION	DATE RELEASED	CHANGE NOTICE	PAGES AFFECTED	REMARKS
0.91	4 Feb 2004	N/A	All	SPP populated into new structure. Core information chapters (1 to 6) nearing completion. Chapters 7 and 8 (Application Notes & Rationale) under development.
1.0	14 April 2004	N/A	All	First release

Distribution List

NAME	ORGANISATION	TITLE
Keith Stouffer	NIST	PCSRF Program Manager
PCSRF Members	Various	Various

Conventions and Terminology

Conventions

The notation, formatting, and conventions used in this System Protection Profile are consistent with those used in Version 2.1 of the Common Criteria [CC]. Selected presentation choices are discussed here to aid the System Protection Profile reader. The CC allows several operations to be performed on functional requirements: The allowable operations defined in paragraph 2.1.4 of Part 2 of the CC [CC2] are *refinement, selection, assignment* and *iteration*.

- The assignment operation is used to assign a specific value to an unspecified parameter, such as the length of a password. An assignment operation is indicated by showing the value in square brackets, i.e. [assignment_value(s)].

- The refinement operation is used to add detail to a requirement, and thus further restricts a requirement. Refinement of security requirements is denoted by **bold text**.

■ The selection operation is picking one or more items from a list in order to narrow the scope of a component element. Selections are denoted by *underlined italicized* text.

■ Iterated functional and assurance requirements are given unique identifiers by appending to the base requirement identifier from the CC an iteration number inside parenthesis, for example, FMT_MTD.1.1 (1) and FMT_MTD.1.1 (2) refer to separate instances of the FMT_MTD.1 security functional requirement component.

All operations described above are used in this System Protection Profile. *Italicized text* is used for both official document titles and text meant to be emphasized more than plain text.

Terminology

The terminology used in the System Protection Profile is that defined in the Common Criteria [CC1, CC2].

References

[CC]	Common Criteria for Information Technology Security Evaluation, Version 2.1, August 1999.
[CC1]	Common Criteria Part 1: Introduction and General Model, Version 2.1, CCIB-99-031, August 1999.
[CC2]	Common Criteria Part 2: Security Functional Requirements, Version 2.1, CCIB-99032, August 1999.
[CC3]	Common Criteria Part 3: Security Assurance Requirements, Version 2.1, CCIB-99033, August 1999.
[CEM]	Common Evaluation Methodology Part 2: Evaluation Methodology, Version 1.0, CEM99/045, August 1999.

Introduction

This introductory section presents *System Protection Profile (SPP)* identification information and an overview of the SPP.

SPP Identification

This section provides information needed to identify and control this SPP. This SPP targets an **extended Evaluation Assurance Level (EAL) 3** level of assurance for the STOE.

SPP Title:	System Protection Profile – Industrial Control Systems
SPP Version:	1.0
CC Version:	Common Criteria for Information Technology Security Evaluation, Version 2.1 Final
SPP Evaluation:	National Information Assurance Partnership
Author(s):	National Institute of Standards & Technology
Keywords:	Industrial Control Systems

SPP Overview

SPP Background

This SPP has been developed as part of the Process Control Security Requirements Forum (PCSRF) sponsored by the National Institute of Standards and Technology (NIST). This SPP is intended to provide an ISO 15408 based starting point in formally stating security requirements associated with industrial control systems (ICS). This SPP includes security functional requirements (SFRs) and security assurance requirements (SARs) that extend ISO 15408 to cover issues associated with systems. These extensions are based on current ISO subcommittee work to extend ISO 15408 to cover the accreditation of systems and the evaluation of system protection profiles and system security targets. These extensions broaden consideration of security controls to include non-technical controls based on procedural and management functions.

Industrial Process Security

Continued existence of modern society is dependent on its industry and infrastructure and its ability to control electrical, chemical and mechanical transformations of materials and energy to produce desired results.

Generally, an ICS is a computer-based system(s) used to control industrial processes and physical functions. Industrial control systems automate these control functions allowing for industrial processes that are faster, larger and more complex than non-automated means. The ICS and associated systems assure the safe and environmentally acceptable operation of a specific industrial process.

The ultimate goal of an ICS is to assure the specified operational, safety and environmental compatibility of a specified industrial process such as a power plant and its distribution network. The "specified operation" may be "continued operation" or "demand operation." For example, a power plant operation generally is supposed to be continuous while an emergency power generator typically is supposed to operate on demand only. Safety and environmental compatibility means that neither personnel safety, nor the quality of the environment (natural or otherwise) are endangered.

Therefore, the overall security concern for an ICS typically originates from malicious threat agents attempting to disrupt an industrial process such as to interfere with it specified operation (e.g. to create a power outage) or to negatively impact on the environment and/or personnel safety (e.g. exploding a fuel tank or destabilizing chemical process to free noxious gases).

It is worth noting that attempting to capture the requirements of all ICS implementations in a single document is not feasible due to the differences between the processes and the networks deployed across various industries. However, there exists a subset of those security requirements that are applicable to all ICS implementations. This subset is the focus of this SPP.

The SPP has been written in such a way that it may be used as the basis for preparing a System Security Target for a specific ICS or as the basis for a more detailed SPP for a sub-class of ICS such as a Supervisory Control and Data Acquisition System (SCADA).

ICS Background

There are several varieties of ICS, but all consist of the same basic elements. As shown in Figure 1 those components are: the controller, sensors, actuators (or final control elements), and in some cases a human machine interface (HMI) and a remote diagnostics and maintenance capability. These components may be in close physical proximity or they may be distributed with great distances (many miles) between some of the elements) depending on the specific application. In addition to these technical elements ICS include a human element including operators, maintainers and engineers. They also have operating procedures and other non-technical elements.

A simplified view of the operation of an ICS and the function of the elements is as follows. The controller implement control algorithms based on a mathematical model of the process to be controlled and the control objectives. The sensors sense the state of the process through measurement of process parameters such as temperature, pressure, voltage, pH, position, size, etc. The state of the process may change due to external "disturbances", changes in the process inputs such as feed material, or in response to action initiated by the controller. The controller processes the sensor information and, based on the control algorithm and desired state of the process, sends commands to the final control elements which in turn interact with the controlled process to affect changes in its state. The final control elements take many different forms including valves, switches, relays, motors, and so forth depending on the nature of the process under control. The HMI provides a means for human operators to monitor the state of the process and the ICS, to interact with the controller to change the control objective and may also include manual control options (for the case of emergency). Similarly there may be a remote diagnostics and maintenance interface to be used in gathering data used for diagnostics, maintenance, emergency procedures or other similar activities.

Need for an ICS SPP

Recently, several factors have raised concern about the security of industrial control systems. First, there has been a general trend to replace specialized control devices, particularly controllers and communications elements, with general purpose computer equipment and associated data communications technology. Second, many companies have chosen to interconnect certain parts of their process control networks with their corporate intranet once they have introduced general-purpose equipment into the process control system.

These two factors introduce all of the potential vulnerabilities found in the network computing in general, particularly if there is a path through the corporate intranet to the Internet at large. Third, for ICS that are broadly distributed a variety of communications media are used including the public switched telephone system, wireless communications and the Internet. There are potential security vulnerabilities associated with each of these communications paths. Finally, ICS are key components of much of our national critical infrastructure including the electric power, water and water treatment, oil and gas production and distribution as well as industrial and military manufacturing.

To address these vulnerabilities organizations are primarily installing security retrofits or upgrades to existing their existing ICS. This SPP is intended to provide a basis for these activities as well as the design of new systems. In either case, the security functionality should be implemented based on a risk analysis that determines security requirements based on an assessment of threats, vulnerabilities and impacts.

System Protection Profile – Industrial Control Systems

The System Protection Profile for Industrial Control Systems (SPP-ICS) specifies the integrated set of security requirements for industrial control systems. The integrated set of requirements includes requirements for operating policies and procedures, requirements for information technology based system components, requirements for interfaces and interoperability between system components, and requirements for the physical environment and protection of the system.

Because the SPP-ICS represents an integrated view of the requirements, special consideration is given to decomposition of security functionality and assignment of specific security functions to sub-systems or components of the overall integrated system. Likewise, the decomposition or composability of the security functionality is also considered. The goal of this aspect of analysis and design is to define security requirements for subsystems or system components at the lowest possible level while at the same time retaining the required level of assurance and security functionality for the integrated system as a whole.

As shown in Figure 1 an industrial control system consists of classes of components for the direct control of a process (the controller(s), actuators and sensors) a human machine interface and capabilities for remote diagnostics and maintenance. Although not represented in the diagram, there are also human elements such as operators and non-technical elements such as operating procedures.

This system protection profile is written for a generic industrial control system as a high-level statement of requirements. It provides a starting point for more specific and detailed statements of requirements for industrial control systems focused on a specific industry, company, or component.

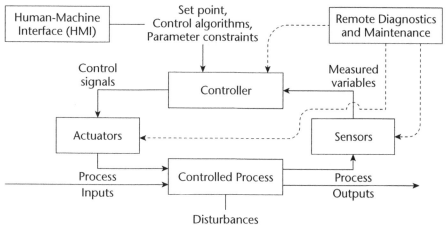

Figure 1   Generic industrial control system

STOE Description

This section provides context for the STOE evaluation by identifying the system and describing the evaluated configuration.

Overview of the System Target of Evaluation (STOE)

This section describes the security subsystem of the industrial control system. The security subsystem includes both the information technology based components and the non-information technology based elements implemented via policies and operating procedures. Particular attention is given to the interaction and dependencies between the security subsystem and the overall industrial control system.

The STOE focuses on protecting data confidentiality, data integrity and system availability without interfering with safety system functions. Data integrity centers on protecting data flows to and from the controller and the other ICS components or subsystems. The STOE is also intended to protect system availability to assure continuity of operations.

Scope of the STOE

The STOE consists of the security services and procedures, both automated and manual, which are designed to meet the security objectives defined to counter threats to the ICS.

The scope of the STOE is depicted graphically in Figure 2.

Boxes with bold red borders depict the primary system security functions. These functions are: user authentication services (including user access control), physical access control, boundary protection, and data / device authentication. User authentication services control access to process control related computer systems including the human machine interface (HMI) and remote diagnostics and maintenance. In addition, user authentication is used by the physical access control system to authenticate personnel for physical access. Data / device authentication is shown as a separate function to emphasize the need for data and command signal authentication. Note that the corporate intranet is in the external environment of the STOE.

The blue lines from actuator to controlled process and from controlled process to sensor indicate that these are physical connections representing the direct interactions that take place. The rest of the diagram depicts logical connections. Security controls based on management and operating procedures are not shown in the figure.

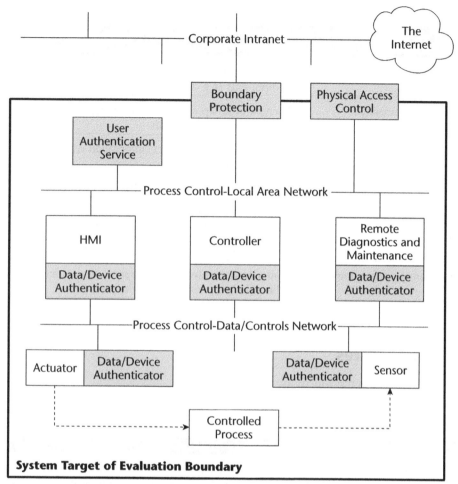

Figure 2   Graphical depiction of system target of evaluation

The scope of the STOE includes the technical and non-technical elements identified in Table 1.

Table 1   Scope of the STOE

STOE COMPONENTS	EXAMPLE HARDWARE/SOFTWARE COMPONENTS
Physical Boundary Protection	Access control for ICS perimeter and control center security
Logical Boundary Protection	Firewall and other gateway security devices (e.g. intrusion detection systems)

(continued)

Table 1 *(continued)*

STOE COMPONENTS	EXAMPLE HARDWARE/SOFTWARE COMPONENTS
Data authentication	Data authentication service performed by ICS components (e.g. authenticators)
Data Confidentiality	Encryption services, such as link encryption devices between trusted endpoints
User Authentication	User authentication service, integration with physical access control
Continuity of Operations	System backup and recovery, backup power, etc.
Operating procedures	System policies and procedures (e.g. backup frequency, password requirements, etc.)
Training	Security awareness & training courses, etc.
Management procedures	Staff selection criteria, disciplinary measures and other relevant personnel security policies

Security Features

The STOE provides the following security features:

Table 2 Summary of STOE Security Features

FEATURE	DESCRIPTION
Authentication	Authentication of the following: • Financial and business critical information sent from the ICS to external systems • Configuration change commands affecting core ICS functions (e.g. control algorithms, set points, limit points etc.) • Users and services accessing the protected assets (e.g. actuators, control systems, etc.)
Confidentiality	Protection of business, financial and control data from unauthorized disclosure (as determined by risk assessment and approved by the data or system owner), including, but not limited to, appropriate segments within the ICS network.
Integrity	Protection against the unauthorized modification of the following information: • Information flows of a sensitive nature on exposed network segments • Internal control data used throughout the ICS • ICS operational system configuration

Table 2 *(continued)*

FEATURE	DESCRIPTION
Availability	Protection against the loss of availability of all critical and major ICS operational systems including, but not limited to, • Control servers • Primary communications channel (or network) • ICS operational system configuration capability
Boundary Protection	Protection against unauthorized attempts to breech both the physical and the logical boundaries of the ICS.
Access control	Strict access control for the following: • On-site and off-site remote access into the ICS network • Externally-visible interfaces of the ICS • System resources deemed by the owner(s) as requiring protection • Those system functions capable of modifying ICS configuration • Critical ICS processes based on state information relevant to that process (e.g. time of day, location, etc.)
Backup / Recovery	Backup mechanisms for critical ICS data and control information to enable timely recovery from system compromises or damage.
Audit	Entries in the audit log of appropriate ICS components detailing the successful and unsuccessful security relevant activities of users and applications.
Monitoring	Monitoring and detection of unauthorized activity, unusual activity and attempts to defeat the security capabilities of the ICS, including the deployment of intrusion detection systems (IDS) at critical parts of the ICS infrastructure.
Non-interference with safety critical functions	Non-interference of ICS security functions and safety-critical functions while maintaining ICS performance.
Self Verification	Self-tests to verify the configuration and integrity of the security functions of the ICS.
Emergency power	Emergency power sufficient to allow for graceful shutdown of the ICS and the controlled process in the event that primary and secondary power fail.
Security Plans, Policies & Procedures	Security plans, policies and procedures covering at least the following areas: • Overarching security policy governing the access and necessary protection for all ICS components • Security management of the ICS and associated infrastructure • Security management roles and responsibilities throughout the ICS management infrastructure • Documentation of the organizational risk management process and its relationship to ICS systems

(continued)

Table 2 *(continued)*

FEATURE	DESCRIPTION
Security Plans, Policies & Procedures	• Business continuity and disaster recovery plans for the ICS • Migration Strategy covering the identification, assessment and treatment of new or existing vulnerabilities (in accordance with risk management policy) during the life-cycle of the ICS • Policies governing the roles, responsibilities and activities authorized for third parties interfacing with ICS components • Policies and the necessary procedures to ensure adherence to identified compliance regulations (e.g. System Audits, Privacy Act, etc.)

Features Outside of Scope

Features outside the scope of the defined STOE:

- General physical protection outside the scope of the ICS
- Enterprise intranet protection
- Protection of "business" information and systems other than that generated by the ICS while it resides within the ICS.
- Primary power sources (e.g. mains generated supply)
- General corporate-level security policies, procedures and training (the STOE will only address ICS specific policies, procedures and training)

STOE Security Environment

In order to clarify the nature of the security problem that the STOE is intended to solve, this section describes the following:

- Any assumptions about the security aspects of the environment and/or of the manner in which the STOE is intended to be used.
- Any known or assumed threats to the assets against which specific protection within the STOE or its environment is required.
- Any organizational security policy statements or rules with which the STOE must comply.

Secure Usage Assumptions

The following assumptions relate to the operation of the TOE:

Table 3 Secure Usage Assumptions

NAME	DESCRIPTION
A.PHYSICAL_ACCESS	In accordance with organizational policy physical access controls are applied at designated physical access points throughout the system whose perimeters are defined by the organization, and personnel with authorized access is documented and maintained. Entry to secure areas is controlled and monitored on a periodic basis.
A.COMMS_ACCESS	In accordance with organizational policy, physical access to communication media, and connections to the media, and services allowed to go over the communications media (e.g., internet access, e-mail) is controlled, as is access to devices that display or output system control information.
A.EXTERNAL	The ICS network may have connectivity with non-ICS system networks through which Internet connectivity is possible.
A.REMOTE	Remote access to ICS components may be available to authorized individuals.

Threats to Security

Threats may be addressed either by the STOE or by its intended environment (for example, using personnel, physical, or administrative safeguards not provided by the STOE). These two classes of threats are discussed separately.

Threats are characterized in terms of an identified threat agent, the attack, and the asset that is the subject of the attack. Threats agents are described as a combination of expertise, available resources, and motivation. Attacks are described as a combination of attack methods, any vulnerabilities exploited, and opportunity.

Threats Addressed by the STOE

The following sections document the threat agents, attacks and assets relevant to the STOE. The last section combines all three aspects into a list of threats to be countered by the STOE.

Threat Agents

Threats agents are characterized through a combination of expertise, available resources, and motivation. The threat agents relevant to the STOE have been captured below in Table 4.

Evil insiders include those legitimate users on the internal ICS network who misuse privileges or impersonate higher-privileged users.

Outsiders include those intruders gaining access to the ICS from the Internet, dialup lines, physical break-ins, or from partner (supplier or customer) networks linked to the corporate network.

Table 4   Threat Agents for the STOE

THREAT AGENT LABEL	DESCRIPTION[1] THREAT AGENT	EXPERTISE	RESOURCES	MOTIVATION
AGENT.INSIDER	Trusted employee, contractor, vendor or customer	Low/High	Substantial	Non-malicious
AGENT.EVIL_INSIDER	Trusted employee, contractor, vendor or customer acting inappropriately	Low/High	Substantial	Malicious
AGENT.PRIOR_INSIDER	Former trusted employee, contractor, vendor or customer	Low/High	Moderate	Malicious
AGENT.OUTSIDER	Unauthorized external party	High	Minimal/Moderate	Malicious
AGENT.NATURE	Environmental sources of threats such as earthquakes, flood and fire	N/A	Substantial	N/A

1. The descriptions for expertise, resources and motivation correspond to those defined for "capability of the attacker", "resources of the attacker", and "intent of the attacker" from Appendix E of NIST Special Publication 800-53: Recommended Security Controls for Federal Information Systems.

Attacks

Attacks are described as a combination of attack methods, any vulnerabilities exploited, and opportunity.

Sources of Vulnerability

The sources of vulnerability applicable to the STOE have been captured in Table 5. Please note that these sources of vulnerability should be further refined by the SST author to identify specific vulnerabilities applicable to the their own instantiation of the STOE.

> **Editor's Note: Table 5 refers to sources or categories of vulnerabilities applicable to an ICS. It is envisaged that the categories of vulnerabilities listed below will be refined by the SST author as each STOE will have vulnerabilities specific to their own security environment in which the ICS is deployed.**

Table 5 Sources of Vulnerabilities of the STOE

VULNERABILITY LABEL	VULNERABILITY	DESCRIPTION
V.PLAINTEXT	**Use of clear text protocols**	**The use of clear text protocols and the transmission of business and control data unencrypted over insecure communication channels (e.g. FTP, TELNET).**
V.SERVICES	**Unnecessary services enabled on system components**	**The presence of unnecessary system services on key ICS components and subsystems that may be exploited to negatively impact on system security (e.g. sendmail, finger services).**
V.REMOTE	**Remote access vulnerabilities**	**Uncontrolled external access to the corporate network (e.g. through the Internet) allowing unauthorized entry to the interconnected ICS network. Also includes vulnerabilities introduced through poor VPN configuration, exposed wireless access points, uncontrolled modem access (e.g. through networked faxes) and weak remote user authentication techniques.**

(continued)

Table 5 *(continued)*

VULNERABILITY LABEL	VULNERABILITY	DESCRIPTION
V.ARCHITECTURE	Poor system architecture design leading to weaknesses in system security posture	Business and operational requirements impacting on the effectiveness of deployed or planned security measures to protect the confidentiality, integrity and availability of the ICS and its components. Poor security architecture may also lead to the bypass and tamper of ICS security functions.
V.DEVELOPMENT	Poor system development practices leading to weakness in system imple-mentation	Lack of quality processes (e.g. configuration management, quality testing) leading to errors in system implementation and third party products such as buffer overflows and errors in control algorithms.
V.NOPOLICIES	Inadequate system security policies, plans and procedures	Lack of formal system policies, plans and procedures (e.g. weak password policies, no incident response plans, irregular compliance audits, poor configuration management policies and procedures, poor system auditing practices, backup procedures etc.).
V.SPOF	Single Points of Failure	Poor security architecture design leading to one or more single points of failure in the ICS and resulting in system unavailability.
V.NOTRAINING	Inadequate user training	Inadequate training on system security issues leading to poor user security awareness.
V.3RDPARTY	Unauthorized access to ICS via 3rd party network	Unauthorized user access to the ICS or its components via a 3rd party network connection.
V.NORISK	Lack of risk assessment	Inadequate risk assessment activities performed on critical assets leading to a poor understanding of the security posture of the ICS and the security controls needed to counter security risks to the organization.

Attack Descriptions

The generic types of attack relevant to the STOE are captured in Table 6. Please note that the referenced vulnerabilities have been defined in the previous section.

Table 6 Attack Methods against the STOE

ATTACK LABEL	DESCRIPTION ATTACK	METHOD	VULNERABILITIES	OPPORTUNITY[1]
ATTACK.SNIFF	Unauthorized traffic analysis	Packet capture tool, keystroke logger etc	V.PLAINTEXT, V.ARCHITECTURE, V.REMOTE, V.3RDPARTY, V.NORISK	Locally & Remotely
ATTACK.REPLAY	Unauthorized replay of captured traffic	Packet capture tool, keystroke logger etc	V.PLAINTEXT, V.ARCHITECTURE, V.REMOTE,V.3RDPARTY, V.NORISK	Locally & Remotely
ATTACK.SPOOF	Impersonating an authorized user	Exploitation of weak user authentication mechanism	V.PLAINTEXT, V.REMOTE, V.ARCHITECTURE, V.NOPOLICIES, V.3RDPARTY, V.NORISK	Locally & Remotely
ATTACK.DOS	Overloading the network	Denial of service attack from the Internet causing system downtime	V.SERVICES, V.REMOTE, V.ARCHITECTURE, V.SPOF, V.3RDPARTY, V.NORISK	Remotely
ATTACK.ERROR	Operator error	ICS system operator error causing security breach	V.SERVICES, V.NOPOLICIES, V.NOTRAINING, V.NORISK	Locally
ATTACK.SOCIAL	Social engineering of authorized users	Unsolicited contact with employee with the intent of discovering user credentials or acquiring sensitive information	V.NOPOLICIES, V.NOTRAINING, V.NORISK	Locally & Remotely
ATTACK.VIRUS	Virus infection of ICS system components	Virus propagation via email system or Internet down-loaded content (e.g. Trojan)	V.SERVICES, V.REMOTE, V.ARCHITECTURE, V.NOPOLICIES, V.NOTRAINING, V.3RDPARTY, V.NORISK	Locally

(continued)

Table 6 *(continued)*

ATTACK LABEL	DESCRIPTION ATTACK	METHOD	VULNERABILITIES	OPPORTUNITY[1]
ATTACK.DESTROY	Destruction of ICS control data, business data or configuration information	File deletion on compromised ICS file servers	V.SERVICES, V.REMOTE, V.ARCHITECTURE, V.NOPOLICIES, V.NOTRAINING, V.NORISK	Locally & Remotely
ATTACK.MODIFY	Modification of ICS control data, business data or configuration information	File modification on compromised ICS file servers	V.SERVICES, V.REMOTE, V.ARCHITECTURE, V.NOPOLICIES, V.NOTRAINING, V.NORISK	Locally & Remotely
ATTACK.BYPASS	Bypass of system security functions and mechanisms	Modification of ICS configurations of components	V.SERVICES, V.REMOTE, V.ARCHITECTURE, V.NORISK	Locally & Remotely
ATTACK.PHYSICAL	Compromise of poorly implemented and/or controlled physical security mechanisms	Unauthorized access to physically secured areas housing system assets (e.g. perimeter security breach)	V.ARCHITECTURE, V.NOPOLICIES, V.NOTRAINING, V.NORISK	Locally
ATTACK.NATURE	Acts of nature causing system unavailability	Environmental occurrences such as earthquake, flood and fire	V.ARCHITECTURE, V.NOPOLICIES, V.NOTRAINING V.SPOF, V.NORISK	Locally

1. The description for opportunity relates to whether the attack can be conducted within the ICS network (locally) or outside the protected boundary of the ICS network (remotely).

Assets

Assets protected by the STOE include those listed in Table 7.

Table 7 Assets Protected by the STOE

ASSET LABEL	ASSET	DESCRIPTION
ASSET.ACTUATOR	Actuator	One or more devices that receive the controlled variables from the controller and feeds them into the controlled process for action.
ASSET.SENSOR	Sensor	One or more devices that sense or detect the value of a process variable and generates a signal related to the value (includes the sensing and transmitting parts of the device).
ASSET.CONTROLLER	Controller	The computer system or components that processes sensor input, executes control algorithms and computes actuator outputs (e.g. Programmable Logic Controllers).
ASSET.HMI	HMI	The hardware or software through which an operator interacts with a controller, providing a user with a view into the manufacturing process for monitoring or controlling the process.
ASSET.REMOTE	Remote Diagnostics & Maintenance	The hardware and software devices responsible for diagnostic and maintenance activities performed on the ICS from remote locations (e.g. Remote Terminal Units, pcAnywhere). May also include the communications mechanism or protocol used to access to the ICS (e.g. VPN).
ASSET.COMMS	Communications Infrastructure	The communications infrastructure used to bridge the control loop within an ICS. Also includes the network protocols and control equipment used to integrate ICS components and subsystems (e.g. Ethernet, wireless, RS-232 etc.).
ASSET.CTRLPROCESS	Controlled Process	The process subject to analysis and control by the ICS (including the inputs and outputs to the process).
ASSET.CTRLINFO	Process Control Information	The process control information being collected by, processed by, stored on and transmitted to or from the components that constitute the process control network

(continued)

Table 7 *(continued)*

ASSET LABEL	ASSET	DESCRIPTION
ASSET.BUSINFO	Process Control Business Information	The process control business or financial information being created by, processed by, stored on and transmitted to or from the components that constitute the process control network.

Threat Description

Using the description of the threat agents, attacks and assets captured in the previous sections, each of the threats relevant to the STOE are characterized in Table 8.

Table 8 Threats Countered by the STOE

THREAT LABEL	THREAT	DESCRIPTION
T.DISCLOSURE	Unauthorized Information Disclosure	An unauthorized individual (AGENT.EVIL_INSIDER, AGENT.PRIOR_INSIDER, AGENT.OUTSIDER) directs an attack (ATTACK.SNIFF, ATTACK.SOCIAL) to acquire sensitive information (ASSET.COMMS, ASSET.CTRLINFO, ASSET.BUSINFO) stored on ICS components.
T.EVIL_ANALYSIS	Unauthorized Analysis	An unauthorized individual (AGENT.EVIL_INSIDER, AGENT.PRIOR_INSIDER, AGENT.OUTSIDER) directs an attack (ATTACK.SNIFF, ATTACK.SOCIAL) to analyze sensitive information flows (ASSET.COMMS, ASSET.CTRLPROCESS, ASSET.CTRLINFO, ASSET.BUSINFO) protected by the STOE.
T.EVIL_MODIFICATION	Unauthorized Modification	An unauthorized individual (AGENT.EVIL_INSIDER, AGENT.PRIOR_INSIDER, AGENT.OUTSIDER) directs an attack (ATTACK.MODIFY, ATTACK.BYPASS, ATTACK.SNIFF) to modify sensitive information (ASSET.CTRLPROCESS, ASSET.CTRLINFO, ASSET.BUSINFO) stored on ICS components.

Table 8   *(continued)*

THREAT LABEL	THREAT	DESCRIPTION
T.EVIL_DESTRUCTION	Unauthorized Destruction	An unauthorized individual (AGENT.EVIL_INSIDER, AGENT.PRIOR_INSIDER, AGENT.OUTSIDER) directs an attack (ATTACK.DESTROY, ATTACK.BYPASS) to destroy sensitive information (ASSET.CTRLPROCESS, ASSET.CTRLINFO, ASSET.BUSINFO) stored on ICS components.
T.CTRL_TAMPER	Tampering with control components	The tampering of ICS components (ASSET.ACTUATOR, ASSET.SENSOR, ASSET.CONTROLLER, ASSET.HMI, ASSET.REMOTE, ASSET.COMMS) by malicious individuals (AGENT.EVIL_INSIDER, AGENT.PRIOR_INSIDER, AGENT.OUTSIDER) via the following attacks (ATTACK.MODIFY, ATTACK.BYPASS, ATTACK.PHYSICAL).
T.BAD_COMMAND	Integrity of Control Commands	An authorized operator (AGENT.INSIDER) accidentally issues bad commands (ATTACK.ERROR) resulting in the modification of controlled ICS processes and components (ASSET.CTRLPROCESS, ASSET.ACTUATOR, ASSET.SENSOR, ASSET.CONTROLLER, ASSET.HMI).
T.SPOOF	Spoofing legitimate users of the STOE	An unauthorized individual (AGENT.EVIL_INSIDER, AGENT.PRIOR_INSIDER, AGENT.OUTSIDER) directs an attack (ATTACK.SNIFF, ATTACK.SPOOF, ATTACK.SOCIAL) to obtain user credentials (ASSET.REMOTE, ASSET.COMMS) stored on ICS server components to impersonate authorized users.
T.REPUDIATE	Identity repudiation	An authorized user (AGENT.INSIDER) denies having performed an action (ATTACK.ERROR) on the ICS interactive systems (ASSET.REMOTE, ASSET.COMMS, ASSET.HMI).

(continued)

Table 8 *(continued)*

THREAT LABEL	THREAT	DESCRIPTION
T.DOS	Denial of Service	An unauthorized individual (AGENT.EVIL_INSIDER, AGENT.PRIOR_INSIDER, AGENT.OUTSIDER) directs an attack (ATTACK.DESTROY, ATTACK.DOS) that denies service to valid users by making ICS components (ASSET.ACTUATOR, ASSET.SENSOR, ASSET.CONTROLLER, ASSET.HMI, ASSET.REMOTE, ASSET.COMMS) temporarily unavailable or unusable.
T.PRIVILEGE	Elevation of privilege	An unprivileged individual (AGENT.EVIL_INSIDER, AGENT.PRIOR_INSIDER, AGENT.OUTSIDER) directs an attack (ATTACK.ERROR, ATTACK.SNIFF, ATTACK.SPOOF, ATTACK.SOCIAL) to obtain user credentials (ASSET.REMOTE, ASSET.COMMS) stored on ICS server components to elevate privileged access to ICS components for malicious purposes.
T.NO_FAULT_RECORD	Fault Detection	Faults generated by the system (AGENT.INSIDER) as a consequence of operator error and/or security breach (ATTACK.ERROR) while performing their routine tasks are not detected nor audited on ICS interactive systems (ASSET.REMOTE, ASSET.COMMS, ASSET.HMI) for further analysis and correction.
T.DISASTER	System Unavailability due to Natural Disaster	A natural disaster (AGENT.NATURE) ceases operation of one or more components of the ICS (ASSET.ACTUATOR, ASSET.SENSOR, ASSET.CONTROLLER, ASSET.HMI, ASSET.REMOTE, ASSET.COMMS) as a consequence of earthquake, fire, flood or other unpredictable event (ATTACK.NATURE).

Table 8   *(continued)*

THREAT LABEL	THREAT	DESCRIPTION
T.OUTAGE	System Unavailability due to Power Outage	A natural disaster, malicious or non-malicious individual (AGENT.NATURE, AGENT.INSIDER, AGENT.EVIL_INSIDER, AGENT.PRIOR_INSIDER, AGENT.OUTSIDER) inadvertently (or otherwise) causes a power outage affecting the availability of one or more components of the ICS (ASSET.ACTUATOR, ASSET.SENSOR, ASSET.CONTROLLER, ASSET.HMI, ASSET.REMOTE, ASSET.COMMS).
T.INFECTION	Virus Infection	An individual (AGENT.INSIDER, AGENT.EVIL_INSIDER, AGENT.PRIOR_INSIDER, AGENT.OUTSIDER) maliciously or accidentally introduces a virus to the ICS network (ATTACK.VIRUS) causing unnecessary system downtime and corruption of data (ASSET.ACTUATOR, ASSET.SENSOR, ASSET.CONTROLLER, ASSET.HMI, ASSET.REMOTE, ASSET.COMMS, ASSET.CTRLPROCESS, ASSET.CTRLINFO, ASSET.BUSINFO).
T.PHYSICAL_ACCESS	Unauthorized physical access	An unauthorized individual (AGENT.PRIOR_INSIDER, AGENT.OUTSIDER) directs an attack (ATTACK.PHYSICAL) to gain physical access to protected ICS components (ASSET.ACTUATOR, ASSET.SENSOR, ASSET.CONTROLLER, ASSET.HMI, ASSET.REMOTE, ASSET.COMMS).

Threats Addressed by the Operating Environment

This SPP has not identified any threats relevant to the operating environment. Organizational security policy P.ENVIRONMENT assumes that adequate security controls have been deployed to address the threats relevant to the STOE operating environment.

Overarching Organizational Security Policies

This section describes the Overarching Organizational Security Policies (OOSPs) that define the broader context of the organization which support and govern the use of a system. These will form part of the basis for deriving the actual organizational security policies (OSPs) to be included as part of a specific STOE.

The scope of organizational security policy includes both the organizational security policies of the organization that has responsibility for operating the industrial control system as well as those for any external organizations that the industrial control system interacts with. Security related organizational policies are shown in Table 9.

Table 9 Organizational Security Policies

NAME	DESCRIPTION
P.EVENT	The organization shall monitor security events to ensure compliance with security policies (e.g. security incident response plan).
P.PERSONNEL	The organization shall have in place policies, training programs, and reporting and enforcement mechanisms such that personnel know their security role in the organization.
P.INFRASTRUCTURE	The organization shall provide an organizational structure to establish the implementation of the security program, in which the policies can be established, maintained and enforced throughout the organization.
P.CONFIGURATION	The organization shall provide management and operational security controls necessary to manage the system's configuration during operations and evaluate and control changes to ensure that the system remains secure.
P.PHYSICAL	Adequate physical security shall be provided to detect or prevent unauthorized access or connection to the system and its components.
P.POLICY	The organization and system shall comply with organizational and regulatory policies and controls governing the use of, and implemented by the system to ensure secure operations.

Table 9 *(continued)*

NAME	DESCRIPTION
P.ASSETS	The organization shall provide documentation of the system and its components, to understand the overall security posture.
P.SAFETY	The organization shall comply with relevant standards to ensure the safety of the system and its operators.
P.NO_INTERFERE	ICS security controls shall be implemented so as not to impede the minimum required operational capabilities of the ICS, and so as to not impede the safety systems that protect the ICS.
P.BUSINESS	The ICS shall be operated in accordance with a business continuity policy that addresses the identification of and response to events that adversely affect the ability of the ICS to operate in fulfilling its design goals (e.g. power outages, acts of nature, etc.).
P.RISK	The ICS shall be designed, implemented, and operated to meet the risk objectives resulting from a system life-cycle risk management program. The risk management program shall establish a comprehensive and integrated set of risk management goals for issues affecting ICS operation, safety and security.
P.ENVIRONMENT	The STOE operating environment shall have adequate security controls to counter those threats originating from outside of the defined STOE. The implementation and maintenance of these security controls should be in accordance with organizational security policies similar to those listed in this table and be selected based on the outcomes of a risk assessment.

Risks

The security risks are a further instantiation of the security problem. The element of risk is captured by the SPP to determine the relative importance of the security needs of the STOE and its operating environment. They guide the specification of the security objectives by ensuring that only those security needs seen as critical to the organization are addressed by the STOE or its operating environment.

Each risk is a product of asset value, assessed level of relevant threats, and associated vulnerabilities (as identified in the previous section). It represents the potential that a given threat will exploit vulnerabilities to cause loss or damage to an asset or group of assets, and hence directly or indirectly to the organization.

Please note that this SPP has not specified the level of risk. Rather, it is intended that the SST author evaluate and prioritize the level of each risk according to their own ICS implementation (based on the combination of the value of each asset to the organization, the impact and probability rating of each threat successfully exploiting the identified vulnerabilities, and the effectiveness of existing security controls). Further guidance on the completion and relevance of this section can be found in chapter

Risk Categories applicable to the STOE

The categories of security risks relevant to the STOE are described in Table 10. The table references the threats, vulnerabilities and assets identified in the previous chapter.

> **Editor's Note: At this level of abstraction the SPP has only captured the categories of risk applicable to the generic ICS described by this SPP. It is anticipated that future SPPs and SSTs will identify specific risks relevant to the author's own organizational context, and therefore expand upon the generic risks presented in this chapter.**

Table 10 Identified Risk Categories for the STOE

RISK CATEGORY LABEL	RISK CATEGORY DESCRIPTION	THREATS	VULNERABILITIES	ASSETS
RISK.MANAGE	Risks associated with the security roles and responsibilities applicable to all ICS users, as well as risks associated with the successful implementation of the organizational security policies.	T.BAD_COMMAND, T.REPUDIATE, T.PRIVILEGE, T.NO_FAULT_RECORD,	V.PLAINTEXT, V.SERVICES, V.REMOTE, V.ARCHITECTUREV. NOPOLICIES, V.NOTRAINING, V.3RDPARTY V.NORISK	ASSET.ACTUATOR, ASSET.SENSOR, ASSET.CONTROLLER, ASSET.HMI, ASSET.REMOTE, ASSET.COMMS, ASSET.CTRLPROCESS
RISK.SECPOLICY	Risks associated with the development, endorsement and maintenance of the instruction stipulated by the corporate	T.BAD_COMMAND, T.REPUDIATE, T.PRIVILEGE, T.NO_FAULT_RECORD, T.INFECTION	V.PLAINTEXT, V.SERVICES, V.REMOTE, V.ARCHITECTUREV. NOPOLICIES, V.NOTRAINING, V.3RDPARTY V.NORISK	ASSET.ACTUATOR, ASSET.SENSOR, ASSET.CONTROLLER, ASSET.HMI, ASSET.REMOTE, ASSET.REMOTE, ASSET.COMMS, ASSET.CTRLPROCESS, ASSET.CTRLINFO, ASSET.BUSINFO
RISK.RISKMAN	Risks associated with the management of the risk assessment processes for the ICS.	T.DISCLOSURE, T.EVIL_ANALYSIS, T.EVIL_MODIFICATION, T.EVIL_DESTRUCTION, T.CTRL_TAMPER, T.BAD_COMMAND, T.SPOOF, T.REPUDIATE, T.DOS, T.PRIVILEGE, T.NO_FAULT_RECORD, T.DISASTER, T.INFECTION, T.PHYSICAL_ACCESS	V.PLAINTEXT, V.SERVICES, V.REMOTE, V.ARCHITECTURE, V.SPOF, V.NOPOLICIES, V.NOTRAINING, V.3RDPARTY V.NORISK	ASSET.ACTUATOR, ASSET.SENSOR, ASSET.CONTROLLER, ASSET.HMI, ASSET.REMOTE, ASSET.COMMS, ASSET.CTRLPROCESS, ASSET.CTRLINFO, ASSET.BUSINFO

(continued)

Table 10 (continued)

RISK CATEGORY LABEL	RISK CATEGORY DESCRIPTION	THREATS	VULNERABILITIES	ASSETS
RISK.COMPLY	Risks associated with not meeting internal and statutory requirements.	TBD	V.ARCHITECTUREV. NOPOLICIES, V.NOTRAINING, V.3RDPARTY V.NORISK	ASSET.ACTUATOR, ASSET.SENSOR, ASSET.CONTROLLER, ASSET.HMI, ASSET.REMOTE, ASSET.COMMS, ASSET.CTRLPROCESS, ASSET.CTRLINFO, ASSET.BUSINFO
RISK.ASSETCTRL	Risks associated with asset classification, labeling, media management and accountability.	T.REPUDIATE, T.PRIVILEGE, T.INFECTION, T.PHYSICAL_ACCESS	V.PLAINTEXT, V.SERVICES, V.REMOTE, V.ARCHITECTURE V.NOPOLICIES, V.NOTRAINING, V.3RDPARTY V.NORISK	ASSET.ACTUATOR, ASSET.SENSOR, ASSET.CONTROLLER, ASSET.HMI, ASSET.REMOTE, ASSET.COMMS, ASSET.CTRLPROCESS, ASSET.CTRLINFO, ASSET.BUSINFO
RISK.PERSONNEL	Risks associated with personnel vetting, security awareness, training, separation of duties and system usage agreements.	T.BAD_COMMAND, T.SPOOF, T.REPUDIATE, T.PRIVILEGE, T.NO_FAULT_RECORD, T.DISASTER, T.INFECTION, T.PHYSICAL_ACCESS	V.PLAINTEXT, V.SERVICES, V.REMOTE, V.ARCHITECTURE, V.SPOF, V.NOPOLICIES, V.NOTRAINING, V.3RDPARTY V.NORISK	ASSET.ACTUATOR, ASSET.SENSOR, ASSET.CONTROLLER, ASSET.HMI, ASSET.REMOTE, ASSET.COMMS, ASSET.CTRLPROCESS, ASSET.CTRLINFO, ASSET.BUSINFO

(continued)

Table 10 *(continued)*

RISK CATEGORY LABEL	RISK CATEGORY DESCRIPTION	THREATS	VULNERABILITIES	ASSETS
RISK.PHYSICAL	Risks associated with unauthorized physical access and/or damage to system components.	T.PHYSICAL_ACCESS	V.ARCHITECTUREV. NOPOLICIES, V.NOTRAINING, V.NORISK	ASSET.ACTUATOR, ASSET.SENSOR, ASSET.CONTROLLER, ASSET.HMI, ASSET.REMOTE, ASSET.COMMS
RISK.ENVIRON	Risks associated with the effects of natural disasters, such as fire, flood and earthquake.	T.DISASTER	V.ARCHITECTUREV.SPOF, V.NOPOLICIES, V.NOTRAINING, V.NORISK	ASSET.ACTUATOR, ASSET.SENSOR, ASSET.CONTROLLER, ASSET.HMI, ASSET.REMOTE, ASSET.COMMS, ASSET.CTRLPROCESS, ASSET.CTRLINFO, ASSET.BUSINFO
RISK.EVIL_ACCESS	Risks associated with the illicit use, modification and destruction of company data or inappropriate access to information. Risks associated with the inability to make individuals accountable for the actions they take when using the systems.	T.DISCLOSURE, T.EVIL_ANALYSIS, T.EVIL_MODIFICATION, T.EVIL_DESTRUCTION, T.CTRL_TAMPER, T.BAD_COMMAND, T.SPOOF, T.REPUDIATE, T.DOS, T.PRIVILEGE, T.NO_FAULT_RECORD	V.PLAINTEXT, V.SERVICES, V.REMOTE, V.ARCHITECTURE, V.SPOF, V.NOPOLICIES, V.NOTRAINING, V.3RDPARTY V.NORISK	ASSET.ACTUATOR, ASSET.SENSOR, ASSET.CONTROLLER, ASSET.HMI, ASSET.REMOTE, ASSET.COMMS, ASSET.CTRLPROCESS, ASSET.CTRLINFO, ASSET.BUSINFO

(continued)

Table 10 *(continued)*

RISK CATEGORY LABEL	RISK CATEGORY DESCRIPTION	THREATS	VULNERABILITIES	ASSETS
RISK.NEED2KNOW	Risks associated with the threat to information confidentiality and privacy, unauthorized disclosure and clear desk practices.	T.DISCLOSURE, T.EVIL_ANALYSIS, T.SPOOF, T.PRIVILEGE	V.PLAINTEXT, V.SERVICES, V.REMOTE, V.ARCHITECTUREV. NOPOLICIES, V.NOTRAINING, V.3RDPARTY V.NORISK	ASSET.REMOTE, ASSET.COMMS, ASSET.CTRLPROCESS, ASSET.CTRLINFO, ASSET.BUSINFO
RISK.INTEGRATE	Risks associated with the integration of security requirements into the systems development cycle and the selection of third party products.	TBD	V.SERVICES, V.REMOTE, V.ARCHITECTURE, V.SPOF, V.NOPOLICIES, V.NOTRAINING, V.3RDPARTY V.NORISK	ASSET.ACTUATOR, ASSET.SENSOR, ASSET.CONTROLLER, ASSET.HMI, ASSET.REMOTE, ASSET.COMMS, ASSET.CTRLPROCESS, ASSET.CTRLINFO, ASSET.BUSINFO
RISK.NETCOMMS	Risks associated with the protection of network communications at the logical and physical layers.	T.DISCLOSURE, T.EVIL_ANALYSIS, T.CTRL_TAMPER, T.SPOOF, T.DOS, T.NO_FAULT_RECORD, T.INFECTION, T.PHYSICAL_ACCESS	V.PLAINTEXT, V.SERVICES, V.REMOTE, V.ARCHITECTURE, V.SPOF, V.NOPOLICIES, V.NOTRAINING, V.3RDPARTY V.NORISK	ASSET.ACTUATOR, ASSET.SENSOR, ASSET.CONTROLLER, ASSET.HMI, ASSET.REMOTE, ASSET.COMMS, ASSET.CTRLPROCESS, ASSET.CTRLINFO, ASSET.BUSINFO

(continued)

Table 10 *(continued)*

RISK CATEGORY LABEL	RISK CATEGORY DESCRIPTION	THREATS	VULNERABILITIES	ASSETS
RISK.CONNECT	Risks associated with connections to other IT systems.	T.DISCLOSURE, T.EVIL_ANALYSIS, T.EVIL_MODIFICATION, T.EVIL_DESTRUCTION, T.CTRL_TAMPER, T.SPOOF, T.DOS, T.PRIVILEGE, T.NO_FAULT_RECORD, T.INFECTION	V.PLAINTEXT, V.SERVICES, V.REMOTE, V.ARCHITECTURE, V.SPOF, V.NOPOLICIES, V.NOTRAINING, V.3RDPARTY V.NORISK	ASSET.ACTUATOR, ASSET.SENSOR, ASSET.CONTROLLER, ASSET.HMI, ASSET.REMOTE, ASSET.COMMS, ASSET.CTRLPROCESS, ASSET.CTRLINFO, ASSET.BUSINFO
RISK.INTERNET	Risks associated with the use of the Internet and email services both internal and external to the ICS.	T.DISCLOSURE, T.EVIL_ANALYSIS, T.EVIL_MODIFICATION, T.EVIL_DESTRUCTION, T.CTRL_TAMPER, T.SPOOF, T.DOS, T.PRIVILEGE, T.INFECTION	V.PLAINTEXT, V.SERVICES, V.REMOTE, V.ARCHITECTURE, V.SPOF, V.NOPOLICIES, V.NOTRAINING, V.3RDPARTY V.NORISK	ASSET.ACTUATOR, ASSET.SENSOR, ASSET.CONTROLLER, ASSET.HMI, ASSET.REMOTE, ASSET.COMMS, ASSET.CTRLPROCESS, ASSET.CTRLINFO, ASSET.BUSINFO
RISK.REMOTE	Risks associated with the connection of remote users to the ICS network.	T.DISCLOSURE, T.EVIL_ANALYSIS, T.EVIL_MODIFICATION, T.EVIL_DESTRUCTION, T.CTRL_TAMPER, T.SPOOF, T.DOS, T.PRIVILEGE, T.INFECTION	V.PLAINTEXT, V.SERVICES, V.REMOTE, V.ARCHITECTURE, V.SPOF, V.NOPOLICIES, V.NOTRAINING, V.3RDPARTY V.NORISK	ASSET.ACTUATOR, ASSET.SENSOR, ASSET.CONTROLLER, ASSET.HMI, ASSET.REMOTE, ASSET.COMMS, ASSET.CTRLPROCESS, ASSET.CTRLINFO, ASSET.BUSINFO

(continued)

Table 10 (continued)

RISK CATEGORY LABEL	RISK CATEGORY DESCRIPTION	THREATS	VULNERABILITIES	ASSETS
RISK.ONLINE	Risks associated with the delivery of online services, including statutory requirements, security issues and controls, publishing and third-party security.	T.DISCLOSURE, T.DOS, T.NO_FAULT_RECORD, T.INFECTION	V.PLAINTEXT, V.SERVICES, V.REMOTE, V.ARCHITECTURE, V.SPOF, V.NOPOLICIES, V.NOTRAINING, V.3RDPARTY V.NORISK	ASSET.ACTUATOR, ASSET.SENSOR, ASSET.CONTROLLER, ASSET.HMI, ASSET.REMOTE, ASSET.COMMS, ASSET.CTRLPROCESS, ASSET.CTRLINFO, ASSET.BUSINFO
RISK.OPSMANAGE	Risks associated with managing system changes, such as changes not approved or audited correctly, lack of consultation with relevant parties, loss of skilled people, and lack of correct documentation. Risks associated with the use of technology for data and system control, including data protection, backup, disaster recovery, inadequate security, and insufficient capacity, etc.	T.DISCLOSURE, T.EVIL_ANALYSIS, T.EVIL_MODIFICATION, T.EVIL_DESTRUCTION, T.CTRL_TAMPER, T.BAD_COMMAND, T.SPOOF, T.REPUDIATE, T.DOS, T.PRIVILEGE, T.NO_FAULT_RECORD, T.DISASTER, T.INFECTION, T.PHYSICAL_ACCESS	V.PLAINTEXT, V.SERVICES, V.REMOTE, V.ARCHITECTURE, V.SPOF, V.NOPOLICIES, V.NOTRAINING, V.3RDPARTY V.NORISK	ASSET.ACTUATOR, ASSET.SENSOR, ASSET.CONTROLLER, ASSET.HMI, ASSET.REMOTE, ASSET.COMMS, ASSET.CTRLPROCESS, ASSET.CTRLINFO, ASSET.BUSINFO

(continued)

Table 10 *(continued)*

RISK CATEGORY LABEL	RISK CATEGORY DESCRIPTION	THREATS	VULNERABILITIES	ASSETS
RISK.IDS	Risks associated with security auditing, security breach detection and response, incident reporting and forensic evidence requirements.	T.BAD_COMMAND, T.REPUDIATE, T.NO_FAULT_RECORD,	V.SERVICES, V.NOPOLICIES, V.NOTRAINING, V.NORISK	ASSET.ACTUATOR, ASSET.SENSOR, ASSET.CONTROLLER, ASSET.HMI, ASSET.REMOTE, ASSET.COMMS, ASSET.CTRLPROCESS
RISK.CONTINUITY	Risks associated with ensuring the uninterrupted availability of all key business resources required to support essential (or critical) business activities.	T.EVIL_DESTRUCTION, T.CTRL_TAMPER, T.BAD_COMMAND, T.DOS, T.DISASTER, T.INFECTION, T.PHYSICAL_ACCESS	V.PLAINTEXT, V.SERVICES, V.REMOTE, V.ARCHITECTURE, V.SPOF, V.NOPOLICIES, V.NOTRAINING, V.3RDPARTY V.NORISK	ASSET.ACTUATOR, ASSET.SENSOR, ASSET.CONTROLLER, ASSET.HMI, ASSET.REMOTE, ASSET.COMMS, ASSET.CTRLPROCESS, ASSET.CTRLINFO, ASSET.BUSINFO

Risks to the External Operating Environment

This SPP has not identified any risks relevant to the external operating environment. Organizational security policy P.ENVIRONMENT assumes that adequate security controls have been deployed to mitigate the risks to the STOE external operating environment.

Security Objectives

The security objectives are a concise statement of the intended response to the security problem. These objectives indicate, at a high level, how the security problem, as characterized in the "Security Environment" section of the SPP, is to be addressed. Just as some threats are to be addressed by the STOE and others by its intended environment, some security objectives are for the STOE and others are for its environment. These two classes of security objectives are discussed separately.

Security Objectives for the STOE

The security objectives for the STOE are as described in the following table.

Table 11 Security Objectives for the STOE

OBJECTIVE LABEL	OBJECTIVE DESCRIPTION
O.PHYSICAL	The STOE must provide protection at the physical boundaries of the ICS to prevent access to the protected assets by unauthorized users.
O.Risk	ICS risk assessment shall be conducted throughout the life-cycle of an ICS, such that a documented and approved risk assessment process is conducted initially, and reviewed with each change to the manufacturing process or change to the ICS; and to ensure that changing vulnerabilities do not degrade the security of the ICS.
O.Non_Interference	The ICS security functions shall be implemented in a non-interfering manner such behavior of the ICS functions and safety functions are able to meet their performance constraints.
O.INTERCONNECTIVITY	ICS security functions shall include the capability to secure interfaces and interconnectivity of ICS related safety systems, as required.

(continued)

Table 11 *(continued)*

OBJECTIVE LABEL	OBJECTIVE DESCRIPTION
O.Data_Backup	The STOE must include provisions for ICS data and control information (including executable software and control data) to assure the ability for timely recovery to an operating state if the ICS is compromised or damaged. The data backup procedures should follow industry best practices including (but not limited to) secondary storage locations, testing of recovery procedures, and a back up interval either driven by configuration changes or a specified time interval or a combination of both.
O.Data_Authentication	The STOE shall authenticate configuration change commands such that configuration (control algorithms, set points, limit points, etc.) cannot be changed unless the origin of the command can be positively established. The STOE shall authenticate financial or other business critical information sent from the STOE to external systems.
O.Continuity	The ICS shall ensure continuity of operations in accordance with a business continuity policy that addresses a known set of anticipated events that might adversely affect the operational capability of the ICS.
O.MANAGEMENT	A policy for governing security shall be defined to establish the following: An organization-wide, security management infrastructure Identified roles and responsibilities, together with explicit authority to ensure operational security within the management infrastructure
O.Migration	The ICS shall have a migration strategy providing the capability to govern the evolution of the control system throughout its security operational life cycle. The migration strategy shall address at a minimum: Assessment of new vulnerabilities and appropriate/necessary mitigating actions to control/reduce new vulnerabilities. This may include maintenance of the current system state (components, configuration, patches, etc.). The integration between computer implemented and personnel implemented procedures.

(continued)

Table 11   *(continued)*

OBJECTIVE LABEL	OBJECTIVE DESCRIPTION
O.Compliance	The ICS shall be operated in compliance with relevant governing mandates.
O.3rdparty	Policies governing the roles, responsibilities and activities authorized for individuals not employed by the control system operating organization shall be developed.
O.REMOTE	The policies shall establish methods for on-site internal, on-site remote, and off-site remote access to control system resources.
O.Access_Control	The ICS shall provide the capability to grant or deny access to control system resources based upon the action being performed, and the authorizations associated with authorized subjects. The ICS shall deny unauthorized agents access to every control system resource. The ICS shall require that each agent authorized to use the control system is identified and is provided with credentials to authenticate their identity. The ICS must be able to include knowledge of the control system state and/or the controlled process state when making an access control decision. The ICS shall include knowledge of time and location in the rules for making an access control decision.
O.SECURE_COMMS	The ICS shall provide the capability to prevent or detect, as required, the loss of integrity of the ICS operational communications capability. The ICS shall provide the capability to allow information flows only between those endpoints authorized by the system.
O.DATA_INTEGRITY	The ICS shall provide the capability to protect information flows from replay, substitution or modification. The ICS shall provide the capability to allow the recipient of an authorized information flow to verify the correctness of the received information.
O.CONFIDENTIALITY	The ICS shall protect the confidentiality of information determined by the respective owners as requiring protection, including, but not limited to, information related to business, financial and control data.

(continued)

Table 11   *(continued)*

OBJECTIVE LABEL	OBJECTIVE DESCRIPTION
O.AVAILABILITY	The ICS shall have continuity of availability for operational capability. The ICS shall be capable of continuing operation if a control server is unavailable for any reason. The ICS shall be capable of continuing operation if the primary communications channel is unavailable for any reason.
O.SYSTEM_INTEGRITY	The ICS shall provide the capability to prevent or detect, as required, the loss of integrity of the ICS operational system configuration and capability. The ICS shall provide the capability to restrict access to the functions used to establish and maintain the secure operational configuration of the ICS.
O.SYSTEM_DIAGNOSTICS	The ICS shall be capable of performing self-tests to verify the configuration and integrity of the security functions of the ICS. The ICS shall provide the capability for self-test to be executed on start-up, at periodic intervals, and on demand.
O.MONITORING	The ICS shall be capable of detecting unauthorized activity, unusual activity and attempts to defeat the security capabilities of the ICS.
O.AUDIT	The ICS shall provide the capability to record and maintain event traces that reflect the successful and unsuccessful security relevant activities involving ICS resources.
O.IDS	The ICS shall be capable of detecting unauthorized activity, unusual activity and attempts to defeat the security capabilities of the ICS. The control system shall be capable of initiating action in response to the detection of a potential violation of the ICS security policy.

Bibliography

The following documents and publications provide additional information on SCADA systems and SCADA security topics.

ABT Associates. *The Economic Impact of Nuclear Terrorist Attacks on Freight Transport Systems in an Age of Seaport Vulnerability,* Executive Summary. April 30, 2003.

American Institute of Chemical Engineers (AIChE) Center for Process Safety. *Guidelines for Managing and Analyzing the Security Vulnerabilities of Fixed Chemical Sites.* August 2002.

American Petroleum Institute. *SCADA Security* (API Standard 1164, Draft), Appendix B. March, 2004.

Amin, M. "National Infrastructures as Complex Interactive Networks." In *Automation, Control and Complexity: An Integrated Approach*, pp. 263–286. New York: John Wiley & Sons, 2000.

Attacking Networked Embedded Systems. Vancouver, Canada: CanSecWest Conference, May 2003.

Bald, G., Acting Assistant Director, Counterterrorism Division, FBI. "Covering the Waterfront — A Review of Seaport Security Since September 11, 2001" (Congressional Testimony before the Senate Judiciary Committee, Subcommittee on Terrorism, Technology, and Homeland Security). January 27, 2004.

Barletta, W., and J. Westby. "The Role of National Laboratories and Universities in Bay Area Preparedness." In *Meeting the Challenge of Homeland Security,* Second Edition, pp. 9–12. October, 2003.

Bellovin, S. *Cryptography and the Internet, Advances in Cryptology.* CRYPTO '98, 18th Annual International Cryptology Conference, Santa Barbara, CA: August 1998.

Berinato, S. "Debunking the Threat to Water Utilities," *CIO Magazine,* March 15, 2002.

Beum, H. "Technology Update: Cyber Security Guidance-Interface Technologies," *Control Engineering,* June 1, 2004.

Byres, E. "Designing Secure Networks for Process Control," *IEEE Industry Applications Magazine,* vol. 6, no. 5, September/October, 2000.

Byres, E., and D. Hoffman. "IT Security and the Plant Floor," *InTech Magazine,* December 2002.

Byres, E., J. Carter, A. Elramly, and D. Hoffman, *Worlds in Collision — Ethernet and the Factory Floor.* ISA 2002 Emerging Technologies Conference. Chicago: October 2002.

CCITT, *The Directory-Authentication Framework* (Recommendation X.509). Geneva: Consultation Committee, International Telephone and Telegraph, International Telecommunications Union, 1987.

Civil Engineering Research Foundation. "Protecting Infrastructure." In *Designing and Managing Vulnerability.* Washington, DC: American Society of Civil Engineering, October 2001.

Cole, E., R. Krutz, and J. Connelly. *The Network Security Bible.* New York: John Wiley & Sons, 2005.

Committee on Critical Infrastructure Protection. *Securing Oil and Natural Gas Infrastructures in the New Economy.* National Petroleum Council, June, 2001.

Computer Science and Telecommunications Board, National Research Council. *Embedded, Everywhere.* Washington, DC: National Academy Press, 2001.

Computer Science and Telecommunications Board, National Research Council. *The Internet's Coming of Age.* Washington, DC: National Academy Press, 2001.

Dacey, R. *Critical Infrastructure Protection: Challenges in Securing Control Systems* (GAO Document GAO-04-140T). October 1, 2003.

Deininger, R. *The Threat of Chemical and Biological Agents to the Public Water Supply Systems.* McLean, VA: Water Pipeline Database, Science Applications International Corporation.

Department of Homeland Security. *Procedures for Handling Critical Infrastructure Information; Proposed Rule* (Federal Register, 6 CFR Part 29). Washington, DC: Department of Homeland Security, April 15, 2003.

Department of Transportation, Federal Transit Administration. *Rail Fixed Guideway Systems; State Safety Oversight; Proposed Rule* (Federal Register, vol.69, no.46, 49 CFR Part 659), March 9, 2004.

Federal Emergency Management Agency. *Federal Response Plan.* Washington, DC: April 1999.

Frankel, Y., A. Herzberg, et al. "Enhanced Security Protocols for the CDPD Network: Security Issues in a CDPD Wireless Network." *IEEE Personal Communications,* August 1995, pp. 16–27.

Fraser, B. *Site Security Handbook* (RCF 2196). Internet Engineering Task Force, September 1997.

Haimes, Y., and P. Jiang, "Leontief-Based Model of Risk in Complex Interconnected Infrastructures." *Journal of Infrastructure Systems,* March 2001.

Holland-Knight Attorneys. "The State of U.S. Ports." *Current Maritime Developments,* March 3, 2005.

Homeland Security Act of 2002. Public Law 107-296, November 25, 2002.

Homeland Security, Process for Reporting Lessons Learned from Seaport Exercises Needs Further Attention (GAO-05-170, Report to Congressional Requesters). January, 2005.

Homeland Security Task Force. *Defending the American Homeland.* Washington, DC: The Heritage Foundation, 2002.

Honeywell Limited. *Experion PKS Network and Security Planning Guide EP-DSX173,* Release 210. Australia: October 2004.

IEEE Standard Definition, Specification, and Analysis of Systems Used for Supervisory Control, Data Acquisition, and Automatic Control (IEEE Standard C37.1-1994). Institute of Electrical and Electronics Engineers.

IEEE Standard for Digital Computers in Safety Systems of Nuclear Power Generating Stations (IEEE Standard 7-4.3.2). Institute of Electrical and Electronics Engineers.

Industrial Automation Open Networking Association (IAONA). *The IAONA Handbook for Network Security,* Draft/RFC v0.4. Magdeburg, Germany: 2003.

Information Technology — Code of Practice for Information Security Management (International Standard ISO/IEC 17799).

Instrumentation, Systems, and Automation Society. *Integrating Electronic Security into the Manufacturing and Control Systems Environment* (ISA-TR99.00.02-2004). April 2004.

Instrumentation, Systems, and Automation Society. *Security Technologies for Manufacturing and Control Systems* (ISA-TR99.00.01-2004). April 2004.

International Electrotechnical Commission. *Enterprise Network — Control Network Interconnection Profile (ECI)* (IEC/SC 65C/WG 13 Draft v1.04), December 2004.

Invensys Inc. *Process Control Network Reference Architecture,* v 1.0. January 2004.

Invensys Inc. *Process Network Security: Firewall Configuration and Policies.* 2004.

Jones, N., and W. Moss. "Introducing Ethernet/IP." Sixth ODVA Annual Meeting, Tampa, FL: March 8, 2000.

King, C., C. Dalton, and C. Osmanoglu. *Security Architecture-Design, Deployment & Operations.* RSA Press, 2001.

Krutz, R., and R. Vines. *The CISSP Prep Guide,* Second Edition. New York: John Wiley & Sons, 2004.

Little, R. "Toward More Robust Infrastructure: Observations on Improving the Resilience and Reliability of Critical Systems." *Proceedings of the Thirty-Sixth Annual Hawaii International Conference on System Sciences,* IEEE Computer Society, 2003.

Luthy, R. *Safety of Our Nation's Water* (Testimony before the House Committee on Science, Water Science and Technology Board, National Research Council). Washington, DC: 2001.

Modbus Organization. *MODBUS Application Protocol Specification,* v1.1, June 12, 2002.

National Infrastructure Simulation and Analysis Center (NISAC). Interactive Workshops. Portland, OR, March 26–27, 2003, and Seattle, WA, April 1–2, 2003.

National Infrastructure Simulation and Analysis Center (NISAC). Presentation on the Interdependent Energy Infrastructure Simulation System (IEISS). NISAC Capabilities Demonstrations, Los Alamos National Laboratory, October 2004.

National Research Council. *Improving Surface Transportation Security: A Research and Development Strategy.* Washington, DC: 1999.

National Security Telecommunications Advisory Committee. *Report on the Likelihood of a Widespread Telecommunications Outage.* Arlington, VA: December 1997.

Noble, C. "Proposal for FERC Security Standards." Presented at the SMD Conference of Software Standards and Data. Federal Energy Regulatory Commission, July 18, 2002.

North American Electric Reliability Council. *Security Guidelines for the Electricity Sector,* version 1.0. June 14, 2002.

North American Electric Reliability Council. *SQL Slammer Worm Lessons Learned for Consideration by the Electricity Sector.* Princeton, NJ: June 20, 2003.

Office of Homeland Security. *National Strategy for Homeland Security.* Washington, DC: July 2002.

Panel on Transportation, Committee on Science and Technology for Countering Terrorism. *Deterrence, Protection, and Preparation* (Special Report 270). Washington, DC: Transportation Research Board, 2002.

Peerenboom, J., R. Fisher, and R. Whitfield, "Recovering from Disruptions of Interdependent Critical Infrastructures." Presented at the CRIS/DRM/IIT/NSF Workshop on Mitigating the Vulnerability of Critical Infrastructures to Catastrophic Failures. Washington, DC: September 2001.

President's Commission on Critical Infrastructure Protection. *Critical Foundations: Protecting America's Infrastructures.* Washington, DC: 1997.

Riley, J. *Terrorism and Rail Security* (CT-244, Testimony presented to the Senate Commerce, Science, and Transportation Committee). March 23, 2004.

Rinaldi, S. "Modeling and Simulating Critical Infrastructures and Their Interdependencies." *Proceedings of the 37th Hawaii International Conference on System Sciences.* 2004.

Rinaldi, S. *Sharing the Knowledge: Government-Private Sector Partnerships to Enhance Information Security.* Colorado Springs, CO: United States Air Force Institute for National Security Studies (Occasional Paper #33), May 2000.

Rinaldi, S., J. Peerenboom, and T. Kelly, "Identifying, Understanding, and Analyzing Critical Infrastructure Interdependencies." *IEEE Control Systems Magazine,* December 2001, pp. 11–25.

Schneier, B. "Attack Trees." *Dr Dobbs Journal,* December 1999.

Scinteie, V. "Implementing Passenger Information, Entertainment, and Security Systems in Light Rail Transit." *ALSTOM Transport Information Solutions,* January 2004.

Stephanou, A. *Assessing and Exploiting the Internal Security of an Organization.* The SANS Institute, March 13, 2001.

The British Standards Institution. *Information Security Management-Specification for Information Security Management Systems* (British Standard BS 7799).

The Electronic Attack Threat to Supervisory Control and Data Acquisition (SCADA) Control & Automation Systems. London, UK: National Infrastructure Security Co-ordination Center (NISCC), July 12, 2003.

The National Academy of Science. *Complex and Interdependent Systems, Making the Nation Safer: The Role of Science and Technology in Countering Terrorism*. The National Academy Press, 2002.

The President's Critical Infrastructure Protection Board & the Office of Energy Assurance, U.S. Department of Energy Office of Independent Oversight and Performance Assurance. *21 Steps to Improve Cyber Security of SCADA Networks*. U.S. Department of Energy, September 2002.

U.S. Conference of Mayors. *A National Action Plan for Safety and Security in America's Cities*. December 2001.

U.S. Department of Transportation, Federal Transit Administration, Office of Public Affairs. "DOT, American Public Transit Association Form Partnership to Protect Public Transportation Infrastructure." *Safety and Security Newsletter* (DOT 8-03). Washington, DC: January 23, 2003.

U.S. Department of Transportation, Federal Transit Administration, Office of Safety and Security. *Transit Security Newsletter*, Issue No. 35, March 2003.

U.S. Department of Transportation, Federal Transit Administration, Office of Safety and Security. *Handbook for Transit Safety and Security Certification* (Final Report). November 2002.

U.S. General Accounting Office. *Critical Infrastructure Protection: Challenges for Selected Agencies and Industry Sectors* (GAO-03-233). Washington, DC: February 2003.

United States Nuclear Regulatory Commission. *Potential Vulnerability of Plant Computer Network to Worm Infection* (NRC Information Notice 2003-14). Washington DC: August 29, 2003.

USA Patriot Act (Public Law 107-56). October 26, 2001.

White House. *The National Strategy for the Physical Protection of Critical Infrastructures and Key Assets*. Washington, DC: February 2003, pp. 33–34.

Wolfe, M. "Freight Transportation Security and Productivity: Complete Report." Intermodal Freight Security and Technology Workshop, Long Beach, CA, April 27–29, 2002.

Wool, A. "A Quantitative Study of Firewall Configuration Errors." *IEEE Computer Magazine*, June 2004.

Index

Printed and bound in the UK by
CPI Antony Rowe, Eastbourne

Printed and bound by CPI Group (UK) Ltd, Croydon, CR0 4YY

27/10/2024

14580181-0001